When Emma Stevens learned her new next-door neighbor was a psychologist, she innocently asked about how to find a therapist for her own issues. Dr. Carol Brenner decided to accept her as a patient. Against a backdrop of the Laguna Beach Fire, the insidious drama unfolds as Emma finds herself enmeshed in an unhealthy dependency on her therapist, who not only fostered this dependence but also used it to dominate and control her.

How could this happen? Emma explores how having been relinquished at birth, put up for adoption, and raised by parents who did not treat her well, may have created the fertile ground for an experienced predator-super-therapist to exploit and indoctrinate her.

A Fire is Coming is a page-turning psychological nightmare, as Emma tries to escape the predators and narcissists in her life—who have their own egoic plan. Not only does Emma escape, she takes a hard look back at how and why it happened. Emma's unflinching narrative serves as a cautionary tale to anyone who might find themselves a potential victim of an exploitative therapist or vindication for anyone who has had an adverse experience with an unethical professional.

After escaping such a bewildering experience, Emma dives into the field of psychology, learning about adverse personalities and the power of a cultic relationship. Emma may have started her journey as a passive victim, but as she begins to integrate her experience, she becomes a brave witness and advocate for others who may find themselves on a similar path.

A FIRE IS COMING

EMMA STEVENS

PRAISE FOR EMMA STEVENS

This book could have been titled *When Courage Speaks*. When courage speaks, the world as we know it shifts because we see things differently. We get empowered, smarter, more grounded in truth. Emma Stevens shows us what it means to be a brave human, a bold writer, and a human being who not only faced fire, but walked through it so she could help others by sharing her truths.

— ANNE HEFFRON, AUTHOR AND WRITING COACH, *YOU DON'T LOOK ADOPTED*

Emma Stevens' book is an honest and revealing account of the cult phenomenon that is not isolated to what social media portrays them to be. This memoir exemplifies how cult-like thinking and behavior can occur on the interpersonal level. Anyone interested in learning more about how coercive control can occur in everyday life would benefit from reading Emma's harrowing experience.

— JANJA LALICH, PHD AUTHOR OF *TAKE BACK YOUR LIFE: RECOVERING FROM CULTS AND ABUSIVE RELATIONSHIPS*

Emma Stevens' brave and compelling new memoir shows how a therapist can use grooming, gas lighting, and the abuse of power in the therapeutic relationship to take over a client who's in a vulnerable, transitional point in their lives. Her traumatic story serves as a warning to recognize when a healer is lighting a fire of abuse and control.

— JANET NORDINE, MS, LMFT, RPT-S

To my adoptee community and to all who have been exploited.

May we all learn to know and love ourselves as we look for home.

CONTENTS

The center
that I cannot find
is known to my
unconscious mind.

~ W. H. Auden
The Labyrinth

INTRODUCTION

S ometimes, the things we fear most often turn out to be not that scary–and things we think are benign can bring us to our knees. This is my story of how something that was supposed to be an altruistic and loving plan for my life— known as relinquishment and adoption—instead set up a series of traumatic events that would launch me on multiple journeys of recovery. I had the choice of whether to be on these journeys or not. By choosing to live my life fully awake, I am accepting the hard work that's necessary to do so. It's the arduous, but loving act of reclaiming myself. A Self that had a compromised, complicated, and traumatic beginning. An essential part of that work is to realize that what I pay attention to becomes my reality. It's the idea that the observer affects what he or she is observing. And if that is true, then I am, and we all are, helping shape our ever expanding universe.

I've written this story for several reasons. One being that it's so darn therapeutic. I have found healing power in giving myself the love and acceptance necessary to write my story. Another reason is to raise awareness for some of the sensitive topics I've included in this memoir. They include being relinquished for adoption as an infant, a childhood of abuse, becoming an alcoholic as an adult, and being abused by a therapist whose job it was to help and protect me.

This is a tale of how I have traveled through madness to find Me. And through it all, I have discovered I'm creating my own life now. I'm connected to me as I grieve, and I heal. Grief, I've heard it be said, is the first step to new creation. We learn how to let something go to make room for something else. It seems to be the cycle of things.

THE FIRE

October 27, 1993

"I can't *see!*" Panic and uncertainty radiated through my body. The current view from our patio deck overlooking the hills and out over the ocean was a sharp contrast to the usual, peaceful, glistening Pacific Ocean. It was as if day had turned to night in a matter of moments. The sun had been blotted out and the imminent darkness was rolling in and darkening the horizon. A fire was coming. Peripherally, I could just make out my next-door neighbor's pine wood deck. I was worried about her. My thoughts were consumed with the hope that she had already learned of the fire that was now raging through the canyon just next to ours. I was hoping she had already come to save her two dogs and as many indispensable possessions that could fit into her medium-sized car.

"You grab the cats and I'll start loading the car," my husband Rick yelled while urgently wiping the sweat beading up on his temples and forehead. "I don't think we have long —so let's hurry!"

Rick and I had heard the news of a fire burning in our city while we were still at work. The house we rented in Laguna Beach was about 30 minutes away from where we both worked at the same advertising agency. As soon as we traveled up the steep, twisting road that led up the hill to our neighborhood, we jumped out of the car and hurriedly walked down to the end of the street. We stood motionless looking out across the deep canyon in front of us. The wind was hot and dry—and instead of smelling the usual scent of ocean air mixed with eucalyptus, we detected the acrid scent of smoke. The fire was consuming the tall hills that lay just across the canyon divide. The Santa Ana winds relentlessly blowing in from the deserts were met with very low humidity—conditions perfect for sparking flames. The fire became an angry red and orange colored monster hungrily devouring sagebrush, grass, eucalyptus trees, homes, and anything else in its path. The rolling plumes of smoke were billowing up into the gloomy sky over the once green covered hills and placid blue ocean. Evidence that the sun was shining was only seen every so often when the wind would blow a momentary clearing revealing its presence. While it was right around noon, it looked more like the gloom of night.

"Oh, no! Emma! The fire! *The fire just jumped the canyon.* Come on, *come on,* hurry!" Rick grabbed my hand and spun me around with such ease and velocity that I almost felt in flight as we bolted back in the opposite direction. Just before we arrived the short distance back to our driveway, a policeman on a motorcycle was urgently bellowing into his megaphone.

"Attention, Attention! This is the Laguna Beach police. You must leave *now!* You are in danger. There's a fire coming directly this way. Take only what you can grab quickly. *You are being evacuated!"*

4

The policeman stopped when he saw us. He gave us his full attention as he repeated his directive. He urged us to not hesitate and to gather our things—*and quickly*. He left to continue his motorcycle evacuation ride in effort to reach all who could hear him. It was an eerie feeling as we stood in the street and watched him leave. Even with Rick beside me, I felt very alone. Alone, and in danger.

What does one grab when being evacuated because of a fire? Photo albums? Jewelry? What will our three cats need? My mind was blank. I burst into a nonsensical mode of grabbing anything and everything. I was clear on needing clothes, personal items, and toiletries, but other items I grabbed didn't make much sense: a large oil painting from the living room wall, some food from the pantry, a small lamp. I really didn't stop until we couldn't fit anything else into the already crammed car that also contained three medium-sized cats and two humans. And with that, we pulled away from our home not knowing if we'd ever return. Not knowing whether the fire that was on its way would devour all the homes on our street, in our neighborhood, or on our entire hill, or not.

Other than the one officer with the megaphone and motorcycle, Rick and I had not seen any others in our neighborhood or on the surrounding streets. We started down the steep winding road leading into downtown Laguna and to Pacific Coast Highway. I looked over my shoulder at the hillside we'd just come down from and saw the ominous blackish gray darkness that was descending upon us.

"Wow. What the hell? PCH is gridlocked," Rick said as he shook his head in frustration and nervously lit another Marlboro. Rick was a heavy smoker. Before getting out of bed in the morning he was having his first cigarette of the day. When we had gotten together five years earlier, I'd picked up the habit, too.

"It's not like we have any choice either," I agreed. "There's only one way into town, and only one way out." When we were finally able, Rick made a right turn onto the highway.

"Oh, no. I've turned the wrong way. Instead of heading north, I think we should be heading south. We need to turn around and try to get to Dana Point," Rick said, looking at me with eyes that showed he was at a loss of what to do. Dana Point was the next town just south from Laguna—about ten miles. The problem of trying to turn around was that all the side streets were jammed with cars trying to enter the Pacific Coast Highway, the main highway that ran north and south along the stretch of the west coast.

The dark sky was a mix of the absurd and the surreal. The hot Santa Ana winds were black and heavy with soot. Looking out the left car window, we could just make out the iconic Laguna Beach lifeguard tower. I was used to seeing this friendly and inviting white stucco and turquoise-tiled tower surrounded by happy beachgoers, people strolling the wooden boardwalk, and seeing the beach volleyball games in progress under light blue sunny skies. Now all we could see were seven or eight black military helicopters strategically positioned on the once light blush-colored sands of the main beach of this popular coastal tourist city. Enormous helicopter blades whirled at great speeds, causing debris and sand to swirl like a tornado. All we could hear were the deafening sounds of the whirling blades of the helicopter rotors. *"Chuff, chuff, chuff, chuff, chuff ..."* Another helicopter was in flight over the ocean as a bucket was lowered to scoop up ocean water and proceeded to douse the massive fire whose ever-increasing flames were jumping from canyon to canyon.

"This looks like a warzone! Like we're villagers frantically trying to flee for our lives," I said. And the thing was, that was *exactly* what we were doing. We *were* trying to flee for our lives. I was overcome with grief but was also operating in fight or flight mode. It occurred to me just then that if the fire were to come down the hills toward PCH, all of us in our cars trying to get out of town may not make it in time. Would we be burned alive? We had just inched by a grocery store parking lot where at least 15 fire engines were preparing, ready and waiting. Seeing the trucks gave my nervous system a moment of calm. Maybe we *were* going to be OK.

"Shoot, Rick! I *do* think we should turn around. The fire is just north of us. We're driving right towards it." I said these words with a little too much edge in my voice.

"Dammit, Emma! Just shut up and let me handle this. I'm trying my best! What would you have me do?" Rick barked these words while lighting another cigarette. He had barely finished his previous one. I was curious to see if he'd toss his cigarette butt out the window as was his usual practice. Considering the inferno ensuing around us, I was hoping he'd use the ashtray today.

In the past, his angry outbursts would wreck me to tears. That day, I ignored him and directed my attention to the cats in their carriers in the backseat who were being so quiet. I knew they must've been scared and upset but they weren't showing it. They seemed to know that the best option for them in this situation was to take a nap. *Good for them*, I thought. I was wishing I could do the same, except that the adrenaline pulsating in me made that impossible.

"I'm going to try turning around in that gas station parking lot up ahead." I saw the opening in traffic that Rick was talking about and agreed that seemed like a good idea. "I might as well get gas, too. At this rate, we're going to run out before we even get five miles up the road."

It was true. We'd been at practically a standstill on the highway for close to an hour. The longer we sat there going nowhere, the darker and thicker the sky became with smoke. We were listening to the news and getting reports of the progress the firefighters were having with combating the widescale fire, which was now reportedly out of control in the hills just above us. Yet thankfully, it looked as though all of us on the road trying to get out were safe for the moment. The fires were moving through the hills and canyons above the main road and the firefighters were battling valiantly to keep it from going west, where so many were gridlocked in traffic.

Horns were blaring, people were angry, and many cars were trying to achieve the same thing Rick and I were—which was to try our luck at turning our car around and going the other direction. It seemed to be the only thing that made sense. Just then Rick took an opening and shot our car into the gas station lot. We'd made it. We quickly gassed up the car. I was surprised they were open amid all the chaos. All we needed now was to have just as much luck with someone letting us back onto the highway, but going the other way. After a long while, Rick forced the issue by slowly edging our car out onto the road until another driver took pity on us. Or maybe they thought they didn't have any other choice than to do so. Whatever the reason, we were now in gridlock again, but going south.

My thoughts began to drift. I had a lot of time to try and make sense of the chaos and uncertainties of what may happen next. It also gave me time to think about my next-door neighbor, Dr. Carol Brenner. That's almost all I could think about.

2

THE MEETING

September 1993, one month before the fire

I bumped into my next-door neighbor at our mailboxes one day after work. She introduced herself to me as Dr. Carol Brenner. She continued her introductions saying she was a clinical psychologist with a thriving practice in a city northeast of Laguna.

"Oh, yeah? My husband and I work at an advertising agency right around that same area," I offered.

"That must be stressful. How do you deal with that?" Dr. Carol Brenner responded.

I couldn't put my finger on it, but I suddenly felt just a little awkward. A little bit off balance. I had always either held authority figures—doctors, bosses—in high esteem, or I rebelled against them. At that moment, I felt exposed. It was true that being in advertising does often require long hours. And I *did* have a stressful job, but who doesn't? Due to her doctor status, I felt compelled to answer her question.

"Yeah, I guess it is." I suddenly felt the heat from the late afternoon sun bearing down on me and how it was making my silk blouse and skirt cling to me. The blister that had formed on the back of my heel that day let me know it was more than time to go into my house, toss my shoes off and change into more comfortable clothes. I felt a sudden urge to disconnect with my neighbor so I could go inside. It'd been a long workday. Dr. Carol Brenner was starting to make me a little uncomfortable. I felt her intense eye contact that she'd not broken with me since we began our conversation.

"Well, have a good evening," I said, turning to leave.

"Yes, I hope you … and your husband … have a very *lovely* evening," she said while continuing locking eyes with me. There was something peculiar the way she'd included my husband in her goodbye. Had I imagined it, or had the doctor suggested that my husband and I may *not* have a lovely evening? Although it felt a little intrusive, I forgot all about it as I walked away into my home to relax from my hectic day.

Two weeks later, neighbor Carol and I arrived home from work at the same time again. I'd thought about Carol's profession as a trained psychologist and how I'd been considering trying to find a counselor. I had numerous reasons why I felt the need to see someone professionally. I had thought that the next time I ran into her, I might ask her if she had any advice or could refer me to someone.

"Hi Carol. How are you?" I asked, feeling more than a little nervous about making myself vulnerable and asking for help. "I was thinking I might need to go see someone. Like a counselor or something."

"I see." That's all she said. And then she continued to stare at me as if reading my thoughts.

"I, uhm, I think, well … I'm having a few issues that I might need some help with. But I don't know how to go about it. Would you see me, or is it any kind of conflict since we live next door to each other?" I felt the quiver in my voice and the uncertainty of my words were exposing my lack of confidence in asking her my question.

"Here's my card. Call me for an appointment." And with that and no more, she turned and walked away.

In a matter of days, I was in her finely appointed office for my first appointment. Dr. Brenner had a private practice and her services were quite expensive. I was sure this would be my one and only appointment.

"So, what brings you in to see me?" Dr. Brenner asked, while making penetrating eye contact similar to when we met at the mailbox. "Well, there are a few things." My mouth went dry, and I was suddenly having difficulty articulating why I'd come. I slowed my thinking by just trying to concentrate on verbalizing my list. "Rick and I are having relationship troubles. He gets angry a lot. He's in trouble with the IRS for unpaid back taxes, and his paychecks are being garnished for unpaid back child support for one of his children from a previous marriage. I'm actually wife number three. I know it all sounds bad and like I shouldn't have married him, but I think he's right when he says others are jealous of his talent. You know, misunderstood. He's a writer." I paused briefly, and continued, "We also can't seem to get pregnant. And, well … I had a pretty rough childhood and I was adopted as a baby. I've always felt a deep sadness about being adopted—but I don't know if it has anything to do with anything or not." I let the last part trail off into almost a whisper. I completed my list while trying not to look at her too long since doing so seemed to make me stumble over my words as I nervously continued to flex and squeeze my hands.

Dr. Brenner leaned in and said bluntly, "Does it give you

pause that your husband, Rick, is twenty years your senior?" Then she leaned back and seemed content to watch me squirm while I panicked trying to find an answer.

Rick and I had met five years earlier, when I was 25 and he was 45. I'd just moved from my hometown in the middle of the country, and was elated to be living in sunny southern California. It was an instant attraction for both Rick and me. He seemed to offer the security I was unconsciously looking for to create a life in California. We became a couple almost immediately after our first meeting. As for his age, Rick had not been the first older man I'd had a relationship with. I had always been attracted to men who seemed to possess the confidence of older, mature men. It was a lifelong pattern I had to try and securely attach to something or someone who I thought could help make me whole.

"I see age as only a number. Rick and I are OK with the age difference," I said, desperate to believe my own words. The truth was that the age difference was starting to complicate our relationship. There was also the way Rick tried to isolate me from all others to keep me bonded to him. Somehow, I thought having a baby would fix all that was wrong in our marriage.

"The difficult thing is that we're having trouble getting pregnant. We've been trying for quite a while now." I allowed my genuine emotions to show as my voice cracked a bit with sadness. I went on, "And I'm also still trying to wrap my head around the fact that I searched and found my birth mother for the first time just a few years ago. And then my adoptive parents found out about me searching. They told me I was cut out of the family and they haven't talked to me for a few years now. The meeting and relationship with my birth mom didn't go well either. It was as if she wanted *me* to be *her* mother. Rick doesn't like me talking with her, he says she's after something."

Dr. Carol Brenner seemed underwhelmed by the news of me discovering my birth mother. I'd gone on to tell her how I'd felt different all my life as an adoptee and had great feelings of loneliness and sadness. I started to feel a little embarrassed by telling her these intimate things and berated myself for having thought they were meaningful enough to talk about in the first place. She seemed much more interested in my marriage to Rick.

"It sounds as though you have great doubts regarding your marriage. Maybe we should get him in here for marital counseling?"

"Rick has a temper. I'm afraid he'd hit the roof if I suggested that." I shuddered at the thought of suggesting counseling to Rick. He had never been physically abusive to me, but he was often psychologically and emotionally derisive. He had the gift of words and had been on the debate team in high school. He was a master at verbally boxing me into a corner. This treatment was so familiar to me from growing up in a home with parents who took up so much space that there was no room for their children. Authoritative, narcissistic parents always come first—and are always right. Rick was like that too.

After a long pause, Dr. Brenner said with confidence, "I'll find a way to talk with him. Don't you worry, I'll handle it." I felt amazingly cared for in that moment. Few had ever advocated for me in my lifetime.

"I'd also like to offer you my home number so you can call me anytime with difficulties. You could come next door. I have an office there, too." And with that, she stood and reached her arms out as if to suggest a bear hug. I complied and let her embrace me. There was an overwhelming sense of love and warmth radiating from her. Just as I was opening the door to leave her office she said, "Think of me as the mother you never had. *I* will be your loving mother. Call me later and let me know how you're doing. You did a great job today, but you may feel the need to talk with me. Remember I have a home office, too."

Leaving the session, my body was trembling. I felt a little dazed and confused with everything that had occurred, but I also felt an intensely warm feeling, like I was being taken care of. It made me aware of things I'd been craving and lacking for a very long time. Actually, I had *never* experienced. Her embrace felt as though I'd fallen down a couple of steps I hadn't expected to be there. I was aware of how Dr. Brenner spoke in a hypnotic way that left me feeling intoxicated. She'd pause, just a little too long, while staring intently into my eyes. This made me uncomfortable and self-conscious. Nevertheless, I was seeking help and found myself wanting Dr. Carol Brenner to be that safe place for me.

3

AMID THE CHAOS

October 27, 1993, the day of the fire

I 'd never had the chance to look at all the storefronts, restaurants, and other landmarks the way I had that late October day of the great Laguna Beach fire. While the heavy black smoke and ash-laden sky made it seem like night, I was able to get a much better look at things since being in grid-lock was far different than traveling the usual fast pace on the highway that went straight through town. The constant news reports on our car's radio told us that while the fire-fighters' efforts were keeping the main city of Laguna safe, the hills just above town were ablaze. The hills were covered with homes, churches, schools, and they were all in peril. Specifically, where Rick and I lived off Skyline Drive was reportedly in flames. The reports were not encouraging.

I worried about the little historic American Catholic church, St. Francis by-the-Sea, where we had been married. It, too, lay directly in the path of the raging fire. Guinness World Records 1992 identified it as the smallest cathedral chapel in the world. It was built in 1934 with rubble from the

Long Beach earthquake. The white stucco and Spanish terra-cotta tile roof structure has beautiful stained-glass windows and the front entrance to the church is covered with massive, fuchsia-colored bougainvillea. The aisle that my father walked me down was so narrow, I had to walk behind him to reach the front of the church where Rick, his best man, my maid of honor, and the priest stood awaiting me.

Rick broke my train of thought asking, "I wonder if Carol and Gail got out OK?"

Shortly after I began therapy sessions, Carol introduced us to Gail, her partner of eight years. Carol was 42 years old, and Gail was in her early fifties. They lived together in the Mediterranean-style beach house right next-door to ours.

One night I was feeling distraught after one of my therapy sessions with Dr. Brenner and remembered she'd urged me to call her when needed. Feeling unsure if she'd truly meant I could call her anytime, I nervously phoned her. She immediately invited both Rick and me over. While Dr. Brenner took me into her home office to talk, Rick and Gail sat together in another room talking about a recent popular murder mystery book called *The Client* they'd both just read by author John Grisham.

"Emma, you'll never have a breakthrough with the resistance you're showing. You need to let me hold what's too heavy for you to carry," Dr. Brenner said with eyes boring into mine and her hand reaching for my shoulder in a firm grip. She then softened her hold, giving me a couple of light squeezes that felt reassuring to me. Maybe I was doing this "therapy thing" all wrong, I thought. But with Dr. Brenner's seemingly caring gestures, I found myself desiring and trying to adapt to being a "better patient."

"I'm sorry!" I said. "I'm not sure what you want me to say? I was trying to tell you I'm unsure of what I'm doing in *all* areas of my life. I'm really *not* trying to hold anything back." I spoke urgently, as if giving a confession, and being as transparent as I could.

"OK, then," Dr. Brenner said as she rose from her chair that she had positioned next to me. She motioned for me to stand, as well. "I'm your mother now. You must trust me explicitly. I can only help you if you trust me. Do you hear me, Emma? You need to trust me."

Trust. Trusting others, or even myself, was difficult for me. My adoptive mother would often say these same words. "Emma, you're so secretive. You need to tell me everything." And when I would, I'd regret it later because of her always using it against me. Her words to me as I was leaving my hometown before moving to California were, "You're going to have to become a whore to survive there."

When I met Rick in the first two weeks of my arrival in California, and he was pursuing me, I became attached to him immediately. He was charismatic, good looking, and swept me off my feet with his attention. Something I badly needed. Rick seemed larger than life and too good to be true.

Dr. Brenner was now standing face-to-face with me, with an intense gaze that felt like she had just entered my consciousness. Her loud silence and rigid body language told me she was expectantly waiting for an answer. I wasn't sure if I felt light-headed because I'd stood up too fast, or because of how intimidated I felt by her. Even though I was trembling and felt frightened, I felt lovingly cared for at the same time. It was a crazy and confused feeling that made me want to run—but I didn't. I knew I was being controlled by her, but the part of me that wanted to be helped and cared for overruled my urge to run.

"Yes, I hear you and trust you," I had to look at the ground as I spoke. Looking her in the eyes felt too dangerous.

"Come here," Dr. Brenner said with a soft smile. "Let me hug you, Emma. You've been needing to be hugged for a lifetime." She then took me into a full body embrace. "You're trembling! It's OK. I'm going to make everything better for you. We'll work this out together," she said while rhythmically patting my upper back. "You just need to trust that I have your best interest at heart—and that I'm the *only* one who can help you. You see that don't you, Emma?" Dr. Brenner said these last words staring at me in a soothing way that I felt powerless to resist.

Rick's abrupt voice brought me back to the present. "Emma, did you hear me?" Rick replied in a harsh voice. "Where *are* you anyway? Honestly, it's like you're not even in the car!" He looked away from the road momentarily to shoot me a withering glance. We were finally approaching the small coastal city of Dana Point where we hoped to find a motel that would accept three cats.

"I don't know! Yes. I heard you," I exclaimed. When he would talk to me that way—which was often—I'd have to fight the urge to immediately cry. This was a learned behavior from my childhood and trying to stay safe from my parents—especially my mother. When I'd cry, I stood a much better chance of appealing to her small capacity to feel empathy. "We can try calling Carol and Gail when we get to a motel." Rick and I were dead tired. Physically and emotionally drained. We didn't even know if we were going to have a house to return to. What if our house was ablaze even at that very moment? By then, I could think of a dozen things I wished I had grabbed from home. It'd all happened so fast. No time to think clearly.

Rick finally pulled off the freeway in front of a motel approximately four hours after we'd fled our house and neighborhood to escape the out-of-control fire. He ran in while I stayed with our cats, Kit, Chuck and Cleo, who were becoming restless inside their carriers. They didn't seem interested in the water or food I'd placed in their bowls. In a matter of moments, Rick was coming back out the front door to the motel shaking his head in frustration and disappointment. The motel would not accept cats. The good news was that Rick had called our office while inside and learned that our company was paying for all their employees who'd been misplaced by the fire to have rooms in a hotel close by our office in the city of Santa Ana, about 20 minutes away. We were instructed to go there for immediate check-in. And they accepted animals! This was such a relief to hear!

Back in the car again, we headed inland to connect to Interstate 5 in order to circle around the widespread fire which was making other paths of travel impossible, and head north to Santa Ana. I-5 was not as jam-packed as Pacific Coast Highway had been, but it was extremely slow going. After about another tense hour-and-a-half of stop-and-go driving, we pulled into the parking lot of our hotel. We were so thankful. It was nighttime by then, but we'd been experiencing darkness since early afternoon when the smoke and ash first started permeating the sky. The news reports we were still listening to on the radio were not encouraging. The fire had not yet been contained. Many, many, homes and entire neighborhoods had, and were still, burning to the ground. The firefighting efforts were continuing, and no one was sure when residents would be allowed to enter again.

Finally safe in our hotel room where we would be staying for an undetermined amount of time—we collapsed. Our fur babies were allowed out of their carriers for the first time in more than four hours and they enjoyed smelling and getting acquainted with the hotel room. For Rick and me, it was time for room service and then bed. It had been a day.

4

FOSTERED DEPENDENCY

October 28, 1993, journal entry

What is happening? The fires are still raging. And all I can think about is Dr. Carol Brenner! I feel like I can't breathe without seeing her and knowing she's OK. Rick seems leery of her and I'm careful to not bring her up too much. Whenever I speak highly of someone, it seems as though Rick immediately tries to sabotage all my relationships. We all get along when we're over at Carol and Gail's house, but Rick doesn't like me paying attention to anyone but him. He doesn't even like it when I talk with my family. It's not a problem anymore since I don't talk to them much anymore. Rick likes it that way. He says that if they really loved me, they'd buy us a house to live in—since they can afford it. Come to think of it, Rick has turned me against my friends, my birth family, my adoptive family, and my old college roommate. I think he's jealous. Sometimes I feel caged by him.

But I'm feeling obsessed with Carol and how much I crave the attention and comfort she gives me. I feel it must have something to do with the fact that I've never had a loving mother. Even though I have an adoptive mother, and a birth mother, neither does a great job "mothering me." It's like my birth mother had me—but I never had her. It makes me sad and as though there's something deeply defective about me. As though I belong nowhere and that I'm unlovable. Didn't my birth mother prove that by handing me to strangers and then never coming back?

If I had to describe the lonely feeling I've always had, I would say it's a longing for something lost. A longing to belong. A longing for home. I stumbled across a word in a book recently that used the word "Hiraeth." It's Welsh in origin and means "a homesickness tinged with grief and sadness. It is a mixture of longing, yearning, nostalgia, wistfulness or an earnest desire for a home that's been lost."

Exactly.

And I would include the concept and effects of deprivation. I feel this is the stark feeling I must have felt when my first mother walked away from me and never came back. And how long I waited for her. Searched for her. Yearned for her. Being so young and feeling the dark hole that was blasted through me. Deprivation.

～

The next morning, we immediately turned on the television news. Film footage showing angry red, orange, and yellow flames engulfing million-dollar homes, cars left on the streets, and the once plentiful eucalyptus trees catching fire like matchsticks, filled our hotel television screen. Tearful Laguna Beach residents spoke of losing everything. Many residents were still trying to get in touch with family and friends. Cell phones were rare. The television showed charred, smoldering hills looking like the barren surface of the moon where just hours before it had been lush timber and sagebrush-covered coastal terrain.

"Should I call Carol's office number and leave a message

telling her of how she can get ahold of us? Let them know we're alright?" I said to Rick. We'd both been too tired the night before to try thinking of how to contact our next-door neighbors. Now that we were more rested, Rick and I were eager to find out if Carol and Gail were OK.

Well before the fire, I'd begun to feel an uncomfortable dependency upon Dr. Brenner. She had increased my counseling sessions to twice weekly and many times we'd talk in between sessions, either by phone, or her inviting me to come over to her home office.

Shortly after we had begun our first therapy sessions, she had established a routine of hugging me before *and* after sessions. But one day, something happened that changed things. In her usual confident and seemingly caring way, she stood with her arms open wide. "Come here." I complied and fell into an easy hug with her. But something was different this time. I became a little uncomfortable at the length of the hug. And just when I thought she was about to release me from her embrace—she held me tighter. I was flooded with conflicted feelings. I craved the comfort and understanding she was providing, but the hug started to feel different. It filled me with alarm and uncertainty. I initiated a slow release by allowing my arms to fall to my sides. And when that didn't signal Dr. Brenner to release, I started slowly leaning away from her. That did it. She resumed talking as if nothing had happened. I'd had a red flag moment, but it was quickly whooshed away by my larger need to believe in her.

While it was unsettling to feel so attached to her, I felt special that she had made herself so available to me. Right after I was born, my mother relinquished me to the adoption system, and I was adopted by a woman who had narcissistic tendencies. Dr. Brenner's care and attention felt glorious. When she'd tell me of her personal life, I felt special that she'd confide in me. Often, she'd mention during my sessions how many of her patients had mistreated her when they'd been given this same "call me anytime" privilege. There was one specific patient named Maria, who Carol claimed had fallen in love with her and they'd had an affair.

"Poor thing. Maria was crazy. She set out to ruin my life. I was so good to her, too," Carol's hushed voice cracked and sounded tearful while her shoulders slumped. She placed a hand over her heart as if there was an oozing, open wound in her chest. "Gave her everything. But in the end, she accused me of awful things and started stalking me with phone calls and letters she'd put in my mailbox. It was devastating what Maria put me through." Carol seemed far away in a painful memory and as though she'd forgotten I was in the room.

"How awful," I found myself saying. "Where is she now?"

Dr. Brenner's face darkened, her posture became erect, and her brow wrinkled tightly as she said, "Probably in a psych ward somewhere! She attempted death by suicide many times. It was all a ploy to make me feel sorry for her."

I was taken aback by Dr. Brenner's words regarding her patient and lover, Maria. Wasn't that against some code of ethics to have a relationship like that with your patient? Instead of listening to her actual words and following my intuition, I allowed myself to feel special that Carol seemed to be confiding in me.

I found myself reassuring her, "I can't believe someone would treat you like that! I'm so grateful for how you're helping me, and I would never do anything to ruin that." My words sounded desperate to me as I listened to myself in my head. I was unsure of where the panicky feelings were coming from.

She responded with, "I *surely hope not*, Emma." Dr. Brenner abruptly stilled, lowered her glasses, and gave me a penetrating stare that made me feel as though I was the Gretel who was lured and then tossed into an oven in the

German fairytale *Hansel and Gretel*. "I truly hope you can see that the special bond we have is what's going to give you the breakthrough you so badly need." And then, as she ended all my sessions, she hugged me tight.

Rick's reply to my comments only moments earlier about trying to contact Carol and Gail brought me back to the present. We called Dr. Brenner's office and left a message reporting ourselves safe and in a hotel. Rick gave her our hotel phone number and then we waited to see if she'd call back.

On the news, we learned that at least 25,000 residents citywide had been ordered or advised to seek refuge the day of the fire. Then the reporter said, "Vehicles packed with pets and valuables were gridlocked on Pacific Coast Highway as multimillion-dollar homes were left to burn." How surreal to hear and see recorded live footage of what had been Rick's and my exact experience less than 24 hours before. The newspaper reported: "The fire started near Laguna Canyon Road about one mile north of El Toro Road. Pushed by Santa Ana winds, the fire reached the community of Emerald Bay. The demand on the district's water system was great. Everywhere the fire was being fought, reservoirs were being drained faster than they could be filled ..." according to the Laguna Beach County Water District.

"Of course now the concern will be gas explosions. I'll bet we won't be able to get back home for days," Rick said, as his attention was fully focused on the television set before him. My husband was a pessimist at heart, so being hopeful and encouraging was not his strong suit. The CNN network had just become established as 24/7 news coverage and it had become Rick's favorite pastime that helped fuel his tendency to catastrophize. "Getting power restored will be a huge issue, too. That is, if there's even anything *to get back to.*"

We spent the next couple of days glued to the news

reports and anxiously awaiting to hear that the fire, who most were now calling "a terrifying beast," had been extinguished. Rick had been smoking cigarettes and watching the news non-stop. I smoked right along with him. I'd been desperately trying to quit my own addiction to nicotine but kept allowing life's challenges to convince me that "now was not the time."

I was preoccupied with fears that something awful may have happened to Dr. Brenner, or Carol, as Rick and I had come to refer to her now. Since we'd been to her home several times and had spent time with both her and Gail, we were all friends now. Carol still had not returned our phone call. Had she and Gail, and their two dogs gotten out in time? Was their home still standing? We had heard a report announce that our neighborhood had gone up "in flames." I started journaling again in my notebook that I'd begun shortly after my first therapy session with Carol. It was helpful to be writing about the trauma the fire was causing as well as how confusing my thoughts had become around Dr. Brenner's counseling. I had felt an attachment she had been fostering ever since meeting her in my driveway a few months earlier. Her words kept reverberating in my head, "I want you to think of me as the mother you never had." At 30 years old, I didn't really see the need to have another mother. However, ever since meeting her, I had felt an uncomfortable dependency upon her. I couldn't explain it. I didn't like it. But the drive to see and talk with her, be comforted by her, was getting stronger. It was as if my need for connecting and attaching had become an addiction, not unlike an alcoholic who's constantly preoccupied with when and where their next drink will come from.

5

CALCULATED MOVES

The hotel phone rang. It was Carol. I was elated. She excitedly told me that she and Gail had just returned from walking ten miles roundtrip into Laguna and back where they'd parked their car just outside where police prohibited non-authorized vehicles. The city was allowing residents, but only on foot. Carol said they were staying at Gail's relatives in nearby Los Angeles. After finding out that Rick and I, and our cats were OK, she blurted out that both our houses were still standing and untouched by the fire. Carol also said that many others were not as fortunate.

"It's as if the fire skipped right over our two houses and burned most of the rest. Let's get together and go out for dinner tonight!" Carol said cheerily and insistently.

I went mute. Not at all sure of what to say. I knew I wanted to see her, especially after being so emotionally dysregulated by the fire. But my thoughts were of feeling awkward about having dinner with my therapist. And this was different because it was dinner out in public. She had even told me many times that we couldn't socialize since a dual relationship was unethical and against the rules set by her psychology board of ethics. I felt confused. Was Dr. Brenner my therapist? Or was she my friend to have dinner with and socialize in her home? And was it that different from how many times I'd already been to her home and socialized already? I admonished myself by thinking surely it'd be OK since Dr. Brenner was the one suggesting it.

"Emma?" Carol voiced firmly, "Are you there? I'm so relieved to hear you're OK. I'd *love* to see you."

"Uh, sure. Yes. That would be great," I collected myself enough to say. I felt a surge of adrenaline that she was expressing a desire to see *me*. The glorious feeling of being wanted, accepted, and sought after was flooding me with a new sense of belonging.

From that point forward, the four of us—Rick, me, Carol, and Gail—were inseparable, going to dinners, playing rounds of golf, going to movies, and we were even going to celebrate Thanksgiving together. All while I paid for therapy sessions both in her office and at her home.

The last of the firestorms, which had ignited into multiple fires due to the hot, dry Santa Ana winds carrying bundles of red-hot embers, were finally contained on October 31. We heard reports that evacuees displaced by the fire were being allowed back into town. What some homeowners would find was tragic. Devastating. Some homes had nothing but the front door eerily left standing. The rest were nothing but charred remains. Moving back into our house was surreal as we saw how little of the neighborhood was left standing. Rick and I stood in our kitchen taking inventory of how little damage our rental house had withstood. We were feeling fortunate that the worst had not happened to us. However, while our house had escaped damage, our emotions had not. We felt raw by the sense of loss and desecration to our once picturesque coastal city and to the close-knit community. Our bodies had remained in fight or flight mode ever since first hearing about the fire days before. It was ironic that what had occurred less than one week ago, oddly, seemed to have happened an eternity ago.

A week after having moved back into our house, Carol phoned.

"Why haven't you called me!?" Carol admonished. I immediately noticed an edge to her usual professional, smooth, hypnotic voice. "I've been sitting here waiting for you to get around to call me. I find that *very* insensitive. I hope you understand and appreciate the extra attention and free therapy I've given you! And all I get in return is your resistance. In fact, I've been meaning to tell you that I've decided you either have borderline personality disorder, or that you're bipolar."

"What?!" I said with a sudden sharp pain in my gut. An all-too-familiar feeling of doom was being awakened in my system. Feelings reminiscent of the fear my abusive parents had subjected me to over the span of my childhood. One wrong word, or one wrong move, could make my parents spiral into fits of rage meant to scar me inside and out. I didn't want Rick to hear what was being said, so I quickly took the call to another room. I couldn't understand why she would be saying these things. It had only been a week since we'd been at their home for dinner, but we'd had a nice time —or so I thought. While Rick was enjoying the new relationship we'd formed with Carol and Gail, he was also skeptical when we'd go over to their home and Dr. Brenner would take me alone into her office while leaving him and Gail to fend for themselves. There was a definite distance forming in my marriage since I'd started therapy with Dr. Brenner. Even more so after we'd had a few marital counseling sessions with her. She'd later tell me of her misgivings about Rick's and my marriage. "He doesn't take care of your emotional needs." Even though I would protest, telling her I didn't think that was true—deep down, I knew it was. And now that she was pointing it out, I began to see it even more clearly.

"What does that even mean?!" I anxiously responded. Close to tears, I suddenly felt vulnerable and unprotected.

"Until you let down your resistance, I'm not going to be able to help you." And then she abruptly hung up the phone.

My next session wasn't until two days from then and I was unsure of how I'd manage not knowing what she'd meant until then. I couldn't talk to Rick since I knew he wouldn't understand my feelings. I also didn't want to admit how emotionally attached and dependent I'd become on Dr. Brenner. I didn't understand it myself. It was a scary feeling of no longer being in control of my own life.

I went back into the kitchen where Rick was pouring himself another cup of coffee. He drank coffee from the moment he got up until right before bed. He'd always say that caffeine had no effect on him. As a result, our house always smelled like a burnt coffee pot. He looked at my ashen face and knew something was wrong.

"Are you OK? What happened?" Rick said with concern, but we were interrupted by the ringing of the doorbell.

It was the married couple we rented our house from that lived down the hill. I felt an instant coldness as they stood side-by-side looming in our front doorway. Rick took my hand. He must have sensed the ominous feeling, too.

"We've come to tell you we need you to move out. We're going to give you two weeks." Their harsh stare seemed unfeeling. Rick and I stood motionless trying to absorb their words and meaning. Our landlords went on. "Our home burned and we're needing to move into our rental here. You have two weeks," they repeated.

We were dumbfounded. What were we to say? We ended up acknowledging what they'd said and told them we understood. I wanted to say anything that would allow me to shut the door. Rick was furious. I was distraught.

"Well, that's just perfect. We have to find another rental. They've left us with no fucking choice," Rick said, placing the palm of his hand to his forehead moving it in a circular fashion as if to rub away the stress. "And you *know* buying a place is out of the question since I'm in trouble with the IRS and all those back taxes. We're fucked."

When Rick and I first met, five years before the fire, he had been living in a hotel and paying cash for his room. He had convincingly explained to me how he couldn't let the Internal Revenue Services find him because of a mistake he had made on his taxes ten years prior. Paying cash made it difficult for anyone to track him down, and although at first I was concerned, I had felt sorry for him and we'd used my credit and background check to obtain our rental house.

I sat down feeling my own anxiety from what Dr. Brenner had just told me about having a mental condition, and now learning of our "eviction." Just then, my white and black cat, Kit, gave me a drive-by against my legs while looking up at me with concern. She seemed to always sense my emotions. I welcomed her up into my lap as I gave her a rub and a cuddle.

"What do they expect us to do?!" I cried. The culmination of anxiety from the fire, the confusion of our relationship with our next-door neighbors, my therapy sessions, and now —our need to find another rental home, pack, and move— everything seemed impossible to process. The weight of it all felt crushing and unresolvable. All of it was compounded by Dr. Brenner hanging up on me without an explanation.

"*Move*," Rick spat. "*That's* what they expect us to do! We can't *afford* to move!" He was pacing the floor, clearly agitated. "Do you know that our greedy landlords intention-ally left their BMW parked on the street during the fire just to claim the insurance money?! And *now,* they're just kicking us out since it suits them to do so." Kit jumped off my lap in a frantic mad dash, feeling the anxious energy.

I took a deep breath and almost whispered, "I'm going to go next door and see what Carol was calling me about."

"Oh, great, Emma! What the *hell* is *going on* between you two anyway?"

I shuddered at Rick's booming outburst. When he forcibly punched the wall with his fist, I was frightened, but also angry. Really angry. "She's my therapist, Rick. What do you mean what's going on? I can't talk to you when you're yelling at me! I'll be back later." I used his angry words as my justification to walk out the door and over to my therapist's house.

6

PUNISHMENT AND REWARD

November 8, 1993, journal entry

I'm so confused. Dr. B is cold and distant. What did I do? What if she leaves me? I went over to her house yesterday to see what she'd meant by diagnosing me with mental disorders. Unfortunately, she wasn't home. As a psychologist, can she even diagnose me? Don't you need proper tests or something? I can't help but feel like she's doing it to hurt me. She knows I have abandonment issues. Things from being relinquished as an infant. Having adoptive parents who thought I should submit and conform to their desires and were withholding when I didn't give in to their wishes. So, when she treats me like this, like I've done something wrong—it really makes me fearful and anxious that she's leaving me.

My next office session is tomorrow. I'm going to tell her all of this. Tell her I don't have this "resistance" she keeps insisting I have. I'll show her how willing I am to work with her and do the hard work that's necessary.

"Hi, Emma. Come on in and sit down." My next therapy session had finally arrived. I hadn't seen her since she'd "diagnosed" me with either a personality disorder or bipolar disorder. Dr. Brenner looked at me steadily with her glasses lowered. Her super-therapist persona—smooth, confident, and in control—seemed to have been restored since our last conversation. I suddenly became aware of her attire. Dressed in a black suit dress and diamond stud earrings, she appeared so polished and professional. I was impressed and more than a little intimidated. I sat. She sat. She stared at me. I was uncomfortable and began talking to fill the awkward silence.

"I'm sorry. I don't know what's happening. I've been out-of-sorts with dealing with the aftermath of the fire. And now I'm upset by what you said on the phone the other day. That I have a disorder?" Large fat tears sprang from my eyes.

Dr. Brenner scooted her comfortable bucket chair right up to mine. I could smell her lovely perfume. She handed me a tissue as she leaned in and hugged me.

I felt as though I could almost collapse with emotion. Trembling, I was losing all control. It was confusing, but my thoughts were that maybe this was what Dr. Brenner had meant when she talked of me needing to "lay down my resistance." So, I allowed myself to sink deeper. Deeper to where Dr. Brenner said my "break-through" would be possible. Releasing all control to her. It felt horrifying—yet intoxicating at the same time.

"Emma. Why the tears, love?" She said softly, continuing to hug me as we sat in our chairs close together. "Tell me."

Anguish and despair erupted from deep inside me. What was happening? I felt completely off-balance and unable to reconcile my emotions.

"I ... I don't *know*," I sobbed into her shoulder. "I really feel like you're the mother I never had. And now I'm afraid I'm going to lose you!" And with this, more tears flowed. "My adoptive mom is and was so *cold* and *cruel!*"

Dr. Brenner softly patted me on the back. Allowing me to talk about things I'd never said to anyone before. Confessing my entire soul. I told her of the abusive home I'd grown up in and how I'd come to California to get away from the oppression I felt. When I'd met Rick, he had seemed like someone who could save me, but now I was beginning to doubt that. There were things in our marriage that were not making me happy—his ever-present anger, his reluctance to be responsible and accountable, or to pay the Internal Revenue Service, and the lack of intimacy. It's difficult to become pregnant when you don't have sex. Rick had seemed interested before we were married, but since then, not so much.

"I'm going to tell you something. I want you to hear me," Dr. Brenner paused. "Are you listening?"

Sitting erect with eyes locked onto Dr. Brenner's I said, "Yes, um, yes, I am."

"If you were mine, I'd take much better care of you." She spoke these words softly and slowly. "I'd take *much* better care of you than Rick, than your birth parents, or than your adoptive parents."

This left me speechless. Mixed emotions. The part of me that needed her to like, and maybe even love me, was soothed. Yet, another part of me felt a familiar red flag alert. But just for a moment. That moment passed and was dismissed. The young part of me that had missed any kind of mothering, nurturing, attunement, attachment, and connection was starved. Starved and hopeful to be receiving what Dr. Brenner was encouraging me to trust that she was now going to offer me.

"Emma, you are so lovely. Has anyone ever told you how

much you look like Jennifer Anniston? You *really* are so pretty." I had no response. I was feeling flattered but frozen.

"Tell me about your parents and your birth parents," Dr. Brenner continued.

Wiping my eyes and wet cheeks, I started telling her my story.

"My adoptive parents haven't spoken to me in three years now. And this is because I confided in my mother's sister that I'd found my birth mom in recent years, and I was pretty sure I'd met my birth dad, too, although he claimed he wasn't. And *that* sister told my mom what I'd told her in strict confidence *not* to tell them. It showed me that my aunt couldn't hold space for me because her allegiance was to her biological relative, her sister, and not to me, the adopted child."

I continued, "I was told I was adopted at a young age, but it was made clear by my parents that I was theirs and there'd be no more discussion about it. They'd say confusing things like, 'We love you as if you were our own' and 'We don't even remember that you were adopted.' What they didn't understand is that they erased my identity everytime they said these things. It messed with my reality."

It was at this point I felt I'd left the room and was deep in memory of how I'd searched and found my birth parents. It had taken so many hours, long years of researching, writing letters, making phone calls—all to search for my roots. My identity. I'd come up against wall after wall of resistance and dead ends of being told by others that I *couldn't have* that information. I *couldn't have* my original birth certificate. I couldn't be told my name at birth. My adoption was a "closed" one that was typical in the 1960's. This meant all records were sealed. Anytime I'd been bold enough to ask my parents about my birth story, I was met with angry outbursts. They'd say, "How could you be so selfish to ask about a woman who didn't even want you and then disrespect us since *WE ARE YOUR PARENTS who have given you everything!* That's a slap in the face to us and proves how ungrateful you are."

"That's devastating, Emma," Dr. Brenner said as my story continued to flow out of me. I was overwhelmed by her attentiveness and compassion. I really trusted her and was determined to show Dr. Brenner how cooperative I could be. Maybe then she would reverse the diagnoses she'd given me.

"When I was a young girl, I learned to communicate with my parents through writing them notes. There was no *talking* with my parents. Their method of communication was one-sided and it was only them violently yelling, screaming, and hitting me. All I could do was cry and want to fold myself up into a ball. That would often make them angrier. I tried to make myself as small as possible in hopes they'd stop screaming and hitting. When they'd finally, *thankfully,* send me to my room, I'd find a sheet of paper to write down what I was feeling."

Dr. Brenner's eyes seemed to light up. "That's brilliant! That was very resourceful of you. Did it help?"

It made me feel so good that she seemed to really understand. I'd felt so isolated and alone in my youth. No one to turn to. No aunt or uncle, no teacher, no person of authority to mentor me to survive my hellish childhood home. We lived in the country where I was essentially only allowed to attend school. This made my home a prison. And my parents, my captors.

"I'm not sure. But I'd write my parent's notes telling them how I felt, or really, I'd tell them what they wanted to hear. How grateful I was. How sorry I was for whatever they thought I was guilty of. How much I loved them. That wasn't all a lie, but I also didn't tell them how much I hated how they were treating me." I remember concluding that I must have deserved the treatment they were giving me. "So, I learned to adapt to be more pleasing and more perfect. Maybe I'd be safe then, you know?"

"So, what would they say when they read your notes?" Dr. Brenner asked.

"I'd slip the notes under their door at night, and they'd find it in the morning. Sometimes they'd hug me and say how much they loved me—which by the way—was *very* confusing after hearing for countless hours how I was a disappointment! And other times they'd say, 'You're a very good writer. I hope you don't write a book someday about how we've abused you!"

"Maybe writing a book about your experience could be very therapeutic," Dr. Brenner offered as she suddenly stood, indicating our time was done. Her motions were abrupt. I'd been immersed in my story and not thinking about my session time being close to being over. Instantly, I felt shame and embarrassment and tried to collect myself quickly. I didn't want to overstay my session time. But then I realized she'd never explained what she'd meant about diagnosing me with disorders. What was I to make of that? I felt deflated. But then, walking me to the door, she hugged me firmly, and to my surprise—she placed a kiss on my cheek. The kiss felt like a reward that seemed to obliterate my fear and punishment of her diagnoses of me.

7

A DAY AT THE BEACH

Several months before the fire

I t was a beautiful sunny California day on my birthday in 1993, months before the October fires and my sessions with Dr. Brenner. Victoria Beach in Laguna was my favorite, since it was more secluded than others, but especially because of its peaceful ultramarine blue and turquoise hued water. The color and movement of the water spoke to my soul. One of our favorite things to do on the weekends, when Rick and I weren't obligated to work more hours at the advertising agency, was to take long walks along the water's edge. At the beach, our stress seemed to melt away as we felt the warmth of the sun and cool wind on our skin. It was lovely.

"Let's take a walk," I said to Rick as I got up from my brightly colored beach towel and tied my swimsuit cover-up around my waist. He didn't hesitate and we walked to the water's edge to step in the incoming surf.

I wanted to share with Rick my concern that we'd not become pregnant after months of trying. Was it time to see a doctor? Should we find out if there might be a problem? I was apprehensive bringing this up since I knew Rick was greatly opposed to seeing doctors in general. Many times, when he'd have an abscessed tooth, he opted to writhe in agony lying in bed for weeks, before finally going to see his dentist.

"Rick, I found a doctor in Newport that deals with different issues surrounding infertility. I've made an appointment." I held my breath waiting for his answer. When no response came, I added, "It's just a consultation. No big deal."

I intentionally veered into an incoming wave and felt the ice-cold water up to my ankles. The hot sun on my skin and the icy water freezing my feet was a blended pleasure. It felt like there could be no better time than this to broach the conversation.

I paused to look at Rick's profile and he responded, "OK, sure. Set something up."

I smiled as I grabbed his hand, and we lazily walked on. Off in the distance a large white ship appeared on the horizon. Then I spotted a small sailboat with its sails fully open gliding in the ocean much closer. Up in the sky was the multicolored chute of a parasailer traversing the coast. Little sand crabs were running to and fro from the holes they were digging that served as their refuge close to the shoreline. Approaching where we had left our beach towels and other belongings, I heard the undeniable melody of "Dreamlover" by pop-artist Mariah Carey drifting into the air as we passed by the umbrella and towel of a fellow beachgoer. The smell of suntan lotion mixed with ocean air and wind was intoxicating.

I shook my towel free of sand before plopping down and feeling the sun make me drowsy. I'd long since learned how to sink my body into the moldable sand to make my impression. It took many efforts of sinking each body part to the right depth into the sand before feeling as though I belonged there. As if I were part of the sand. On this beach. Right then. Just being present. The warm sun, cool breeze from the ocean, and the sound of the crashing waves were seductively soothing. I was also letting my thoughts float in anticipation of scheduling the doctor's appointment. The one that might bring Rick and I closer to becoming pregnant. And then, sleep overtook me.

I awoke feeling hot. I made my way to my feet and walked the few steps to the water's edge. A satisfying cooling down happened almost instantly as I stood in the gentle moving water of the incoming waves. I glanced behind me to see Rick coming to join me. And then, unexpectedly, in my peripheral vision I detected movement of something black and sleek rolling through the surface of the water not more than 20 feet away. No, I thought. It was just the large black rocks that were exposed at the surface of the water. I kept staring. Rick was right beside me then.

"Rick?! What *is* that?" I asked rhetorically. I kept wondering if my eyes were playing a trick on me. "Oh my gosh, Rick! Are those ... *whales?!*"

By then, there was no denying we were witnessing an amazingly beautiful pod of whales that were so close, we could have almost reached out and touched them. The pod included several calves, and their mother, the cow. We stood in amazement. Our jaws dropped open. Unsure we were seeing what we were seeing. And no one else on the crowded beach appeared to notice. The whole scene of the sleek, shiny, black-skinned whales breaking the water and rolling through the shallow waters lasted only moments. And then they were gone. Beautiful. Happy birthday to me. I took it as a sign of my impending motherhood.

8

A MARRIAGE UNDER ATTACK

The mandate for Rick and me to move from our rental home so the landlords could reside there was chipping away at my ability to think logically and clearly. Dr. Brenner had convinced me that Rick did not have my best interest at heart and that having a baby with him would be disastrous. During one of our marital sessions with Dr. Brenner, she asked Rick, "How old are your children from your previous marriages? How often do you see them?" I saw the color drain from Rick's face.

"I don't have a relationship with either of them. Both of their mothers turned them against me. It's complicated." I could tell this was a conversation Rick did not want to be having.

"Have you been vulnerable and tried to have a relationship with them?" Dr. Brenner probed.

"Yes, I've tried. It's just not going to work." And with that, Rick shut down and refused to answer any more personal questions.

Later, in another session with just me, Dr. Brenner

brought up this conversation with Rick as support that my marriage was not going to survive.

With her bucket chair practically touching mine, Dr. Brenner placed her well-manicured hand out and touched my arm. I succumbed to her swift confident movements engaging me to listen. "I think you know he's not right for you. He doesn't 'own his stuff.' He blames everyone else for his failings. He clearly doesn't have your best interest at heart, dear Emma." Dr. Brenner was speaking slowly and mesmerizing me with that penetrating eye contact that I'd become familiar with, but which was nonetheless unnerving.

With her words, I felt my world unraveling, as if life as I knew it had just lost all shape and form. I trusted Dr. Brenner and had become deeply attached to her. Her opinion mattered. In that moment I felt fear and anguish overtake me. It was an old fear of abandonment. Abandonment from everyone and everything I'd ever known. Dr. Brenner instilling this alarm in me regarding my marriage was enough to trigger these deepest fears in me. It's as if the gates of doubt had been opened and I was believing this professional's assessment regarding my life. The ground beneath my feet felt far from solid and my balance compromised. I couldn't deny there were problems in my marriage to Rick. There were intimacy problems that I'd asked him to seek medical help for—to no avail. This was one reason getting pregnant was eluding us. Rick did not like doctors. Other issues included his avoidance of paying federal income taxes and back child support payments, along with other responsibilities he continually neglected and intentionally avoided. He'd allow a problem to become insurmountable before taking any action at all. But to allow myself to come out of the denial of believing there was anything seriously wrong in my marriage would be to face the cold harsh truth that my life was precariously built no stronger than a house of cards.

Dr. Brenner was still focused on my face as she scooched to the edge of her cushioned, mauve-colored bucket-style chair to where her knees were now touching mine. She was dressed in an expensive looking feminine, yet masculine suit jacket and skirt, black pumps, and wore an intoxicating perfume. I felt an electric current shoot through me. She was in my personal space.

Red flag.

Then the red flag was dismissed.

Instead of being alarmed, I chose to think that this doctor cared about me so much she didn't want me to be making a huge life mistake. I felt special and maybe even worth her attention. My thinking began lining up with hers and I felt safe to face certain issues about my life since Dr. Brenner was there to make me feel safe and not so alone.

Later that day, after my long day at work and another emotionally draining session with Dr. Brenner, Rick was waiting for me in our kitchen smoking a cigarette.

"Where've you been?" Rick said in a curt, accusatory manner. His brow was scrunched and looked as though the smoke from his cigarette was getting into his half-squinted eyes. It made him look a little like the actor, Clint Eastwood, saying "Go ahead, make my day."

"Work. How about you?" I didn't like his tone. Or how it often felt as though he was trying to control me. It gave me an oppressive feeling similar to my life growing up with my parents. Unable to have my own opinions or set my own boundaries. Screw them, I thought. I can make my own decisions and I don't have to answer to any of them.

"I was just asking." Rick looked away and his energy seemed to change and became more pleasant. "Carol and

Gail want to know if we'd like to have dinner at their place tonight."

Hearing this, I felt a rush of excitement. It was clear even to me that I was obsessed with Carol. But I was also still very confused by whether Carol was my friend, or was Dr. Brenner my doctor? All I knew was that I only felt alive and OK when I was with her. In any capacity. Careful not to expose how my heartrate had just spiked at the thought of seeing Dr. Brenner, I answered, "Sure. That sounds great."

"K," Rick answered. "How'd it go to find us a new rental?"

I had not yet had a chance, or the mental capacity to face finding us a new rental. The two-week move-out timeframe given us by our landlords was ending soon. I had done nothing to aid in our upcoming move. "Rick, we're going to *have* to ask for an extension. Life has been so crazy! I haven't had the time to look for anything yet." I remarked as I felt an internal heat begin to boil within me.

"What the hell have you been doing then? I *told* you to get on it! These people are *not* going to give us an extension—you know that! What the hell is wrong with you?!" Rick slapped the table with his open hand and then forcefully stubbed out his cigarette in the messy, overflowing ashtray.

At that moment, all my circuits jammed. I placed my head in my hands as if it were going to explode.

"Well, this is just great. All you can do is cry? I'm going to …" Rick was interrupted by the ringing of our telephone. He answered quickly and then angrily held out the receiver. "It's *Carol*. Maybe you'll talk to *her*." He handed me the phone and stomped out of the room.

"Hello?" I managed through a choked voice.

"What's wrong, Emma? Tell me what's wrong!? Carol was using her professional Dr. Brenner voice. I had come to be able to differentiate between her different voices. Her doctor's voice seemed to immediately make me feel like her patient. As if I were suddenly in a therapy session.

"I hear your distress. I'm coming over," Carol said and ended the phone call. She was at my front door in minutes.

As soon as I opened the door, she led me to a bench in the foyer and guided me with her hands to take a seat. I blurted out, "It's everything! I'm overwhelmed by *all* of it! The fire … the fact that we have to move and find another place … and *Rick!* He's being impossible!" I blurted it all out like a volcano needing to relieve the built-up pressure.

"OK," Dr. Brenner said in her regulated smooth and soothing psychologist voice, "Let's take a breath, shall we?" She wrapped her arms around me as she rocked me gently back and forth like a child. I felt my body and spirit crumple into her seemingly capable hands.

9

THE PREDATOR CAN ALWAYS
SPOT THE UNPROTECTED

November 19, 1993, journal entry

Dr. Brenner solved everything. She called our landlords and bought us another two weeks. Thank goodness. Maybe I'll have the chance to breathe now. She really was terrific how she just picked up the phone and called them. Didn't even give them the chance to say no. I was impressed and felt very taken care of by her—unlike Rick. It's like he's become my enemy. Maybe Dr. Brenner is right about my marriage to Rick. Maybe he really doesn't know how to take care of me. She said she'd take much better care of me if she had the chance. And I believe her! I've really grown to love and trust her. I now wonder what I'd ever do without her. That fear of abandonment is always a spirit that hangs around me. I'm sure it's adoption related. Someday, I'm really going to need to get to the bottom of my sadness surrounding being an adoptee.

It didn't even seem to help solve my feelings around being adopted when I searched and found my birth mother. I thought I'd found my birth father, but I guess not. He said his name being on my original birth certificate was only there because he was "helping out a friend." But meeting my birth mother only confused

me more. It was like she wanted me to take care of her. I can't do
that. Nor do I want to.

～

At my next session with Dr. Brenner, I was surprised to learn an intimate detail about her life with Gail. Rick and I liked her and thought that Carol and Gail were fun to be with and seemed like a well-matched couple.

"Gail and I are not as happy together as you might think." Dr. Brenner went on, "Just like with you and Rick, there are things that make me know our relationship won't last."

She had said negative things about my marriage before, but nevertheless, I felt punched in the gut again. Was I ready to face this? Did I have to? I'd come so far in trying to create a new life in California away from the horror and oppression of my childhood. I felt that if I allowed myself to question staying with Rick, it may unravel the entire life I had created.

And then there was the bomb she'd just dropped about her personal relationship with Gail. Did Gail know anything about this? Suddenly, I felt as though I was in the middle of a conspiracy. One that I hadn't wanted or agreed to have any part of.

"I can see I've upset you. It's sad and difficult to admit when things don't work out ... like your marriage to Rick. But I want you to remember—I'm here for you. You trust me, don't you?" Lowering her stylish professional eyeglasses, she leaned forward and looked into my eyes with a penetrating intensity. *Red flag.* My insides began to quake. I fought the urge to bolt for the door. Instead, I just stared back.

Dr. Brenner stood and gently grabbed both my hands, which put me in a surreal dreamlike state. *Red flag.* I stood with her, even though my wobbly legs and quivering body felt as though they were going to betray me. I felt a confident and insistent energy radiating from her as she drew me in close. *Red Flag.* And then she took me into her full embrace and kissed me on the lips.

I was overcome by an all too familiar trauma response of "freeze" mode. I felt my mind and body being flooded by knowing nothing other than to shut down. What I didn't know then, but is irrefutable now, is the knowingness that fairy-tale Gretel had just been placed into the hot, inescapable oven that her seemingly-friendly captor had been planning all along.

"Come over tonight. Bring Rick. We don't want him getting suspicious. See you at 8:00 at my place." Dr. Brenner ushered me to the door. My freeze mode was replaced by "fawn" mode to further protect myself. It seemed crucial to not say or do anything that would upset her or seem as though I was rejecting her. However, inside my head was the reverberating question—***what just happened?!***

Once outside in the bright midday sunshine, I didn't know how I could possibly drive back to work, since that would require a focus that was suddenly eluding me. My skin felt on fire and smelled of her perfume where she had touched me and handled me as if I was a newly purchased expensive piece of art.

What I didn't know then was the power of oxytocin, the hormone that functions as a neurotransmitter in the brain. "It's thought to be a driving force behind attraction and care-giving, and even controls key aspects of the reproductive system, childbirth, and lactation. Oxytocin has earned the nickname 'the cuddle' or 'love hormone,'" as stated by Randy Bressler, PsyD., clinical psychologist and author. The neuro-biological developmental stage that had been interrupted in my birthing process and relinquishment (because of being separated from my mother), left me oxytocin deprived. This normal and necessary process had been thwarted in my birth and thereafter. Is it any wonder that for most of my life I've been walking around like the baby bird in *Are You My Mother?* a popular children's book written by P. D. Eastman in 1960. In it, a newly hatched bird is searching for his mother who had gone to find food for him. The baby bird asks everyone he encounters if they are his mother. The baby bird's search for his mother is relentless until he is finally united with his mother. It was as if I were that little bird looking everywhere for an attachment that being oxytocin deprived so early in life had created in me.

The research, self-education, and unearthing of the truth of what had happened to me came later. Decades later.

Rick and I had dinner at Carol and Gail's that same night. Carol served us a home cooked meal of baked chicken breast with a light mushroom cream sauce paired with a mixed green salad sprinkled with almonds and cranberries. We talked of the aftermath of the Laguna Beach fire and how devastating it'd been for our small coastal city. Many residences would have to be rebuilt and the progress of getting all the reconstruction started was proving to be extremely slow. It was dawning on us that our city's restoration toward returning to normal was going to be years ahead.

"Emma, are you doing alright? You seem quiet tonight," Carol had probed. Everyone looked at me. This sudden attention horrified me. Shooting pains of self-consciousness flooded my system causing my skin to feel as though it was pulsating bright red. With the sudden knowingness that I was on the edge of a floodgate of tears, I pushed back from the table and dashed to the bathroom. This was my flight response. This sense of panic was familiar. As a child, I had learned to cope with my parent's emotional outbursts, psychological and physical abuse by being in a constant state of fight or flight. I had learned to sense the signs of danger. I'd also developed an automatic response of crying whenever I sensed this impending doom. What I was feeling at Carol and Gail's table that night had triggered that same childhood behavior within me. It was that, and it was coupled with the disturbing fact that Dr. Brenner had kissed me on the mouth and pressed her breasts into my chest earlier that day in my therapy session.

10

THE PSYCHE SPLIT

Carol caught me right before I'd been able to close the bathroom door behind me—hoping to shut everyone and everything out.

"Come, Emma. I've told Rick and Gail that you and I need to have a session. They're fine in the other room. Let's go downstairs for privacy." She led me downstairs to where her home office was as I cried; I could barely see to take my next step. Carol was practically carrying me as she walked us right past her office and into another room. Her bedroom.

My world felt as though it had tilted. Slanted. Another familiar feeling from my childhood was to dissociate. A coping mechanism that I unknowing used to keep me safe from harm. Processing and understanding what was happening with this seduction from Dr. Brenner was too much for my brain and nervous system to endure. I knew I should be pulling away and resisting her attempts to foster this dependency upon her, but my need to be close to her was greater than the sense of danger that was screaming inside my head.

She sat beside me on the edge of her bed and placed her

arms around my slumped shoulders. She whispered in my ear, *"Shhh. Let it happen."* I cried more tears. "That's it, Emma. Let it all go. I'm here to help you through it all. You can trust me, dear heart." Dr. Brenner wiped my tears and gave me some water. She stroked my hair back from my worried forehead and I began feeling my body relax.

I had found my voice enough to squeak out, "What's happening?"

"Love. That's what's happening," Dr. Brenner said with her convincing super-therapist voice. "No more resistance, Emma. You've never been cared for before, so you aren't familiar with the feeling. You need to lay down your resistance and let it happen ... *just let it happen ...*"

I learned many years later that the definition of a "super-therapist," as defined in the book *Take Back Your Life* by Lalich and Landau 2021, is "a cult leader (or therapist) who is self-proclaimed and omniscient, with unique insights. Practices and techniques include isolating their patients, use of fatigue to exert control over their patients, intense probing into personal life and thoughts, altered states brought about by hypnosis and other trance-induction mechanisms, shame and intimidation, verbal abuse, use of thought-reform techniques, and use of charm for manipulation." These are but a few of the techniques describing this kind of therapist.

With my body trembling and in high alert, I was frozen in submission. I allowed her to stand me with my back against her bedroom wall while she stood inches from my face. With swift seductive precision, she enveloped my body in a slow, sensuous light brushing up with her body against mine until her mouth was caressing my ear. She pressed her body harder into mine as she found my mouth again, just as she had earlier that day in her office. I felt myself melting into her embrace and I kissed her back.

Dr. Brenner's attention, her loving nature, her hugs, all of her "love bombing" seemed to be filling a deep need within me to feel loved. I convinced myself that I wanted this relationship more than anything. I even began to feel as though my life depended upon it. It felt vital to me to ignore all other thoughts of fear and to attach instead wholeheartedly to Dr. Brenner. My sense of agency over my life, I tried to convince myself, was totally in my control and that I was in this relationship of my own free will. Each time an invasive, nagging red flag of a thought entered my mind—I'd whoosh it away.

Carol suddenly drew back from kissing and groping me to say, "Emma, you know you can't mention our relationship to *anyone*—right?!"

"Of course, not," I said with my fawn-like reflex. I didn't want to say or do anything that would not be pleasing to Dr. Brenner.

"Good. Because many would say that this is unethical—what we're doing. But you and I know *this* is different. We *love* each other. There's a difference!" Carol said with conviction.

Did she just say she *loved* me? This thought flooded me, giving me a warm glow. Even though it felt wrong—somehow, it also seemed right. Trying to reconcile these two opposing feelings was making my psyche feel cracked. I tried assiduously to ignore it, even though it was chipping away at my core. What my conscious didn't know but my unconscious did, was that I was splitting myself off from my body and soul—a cognitive dissonance.

"I sometimes write about how much you mean to me. In a journal. You know, how much I love you," I added as I broke eye contact and quickly looked down at the ground.

"What? *That's* not good! You're going to have to let me read that! I can't risk someone seeing that and getting me in trouble *again*." Carol's eyes had suddenly transformed into red hot flames. Oh, shit! I thought. I've really made her mad.

I was trying to think quickly of how to get out of this. Who was this? Her whole demeanor had changed. It didn't sound or look like the understanding-smooth-talking Dr. Brenner I knew. Nor was it the friendly-you-can-tell-me-anything Carol. I became frightened and unsure of who this was or what she'd do next.

"I just meant that I sometimes write about my life, and love, and stuff ..." I stammered. "I *never* mention you by name!" I lied.

And in an instant, the Dr. Brenner I knew was back. Calm and collected. She said in a soft, soothing voice, "Of course, of course, but just to be safe, I'd like you to show me this journal, OK?"

"Uh, OK. I'm sorry. I'd never do anything to hurt you," I said in tears. I was so relieved when she no longer seemed mad and that I could recognize her again. For a moment, she seemed to have turned into a monster. Dr. Brenner's next words hit me between the eyes.

"I've decided to ask Gail to leave. I did an unbelievable thing by placing her on the title to this house even though I put forth most of the money for it. I'm not happy with her—and I'm going to tell her it's over." Carol seemed serious. She looked expectantly at me as if waiting for my opinion.

"I see." That's all I could think of to say. It was all happening too fast. I felt as if the walls were closing in on me again, the same way I'd felt upstairs when we had been with Rick and Gail. I was unsure of how much more emotional upheaval I could take. The overwhelming feeling of being off-balance was already taking a toll on me. I wasn't sleeping well or eating much of anything. The stress and anxiety of it all had hit me in my gut. I'd already taken many sick days from work from feeling unable to cope with everyday life.

"Emma, you *know* you shouldn't make this upcoming move with Rick. You should take this opportunity and make a clean break from him. You could come and live here with me." Dr. Brenner's words hung in the air like a vapor I was being forced to breathe in. My world tilted again. Another degree. A degree that felt even more dangerous than Dr. Brenner touching, kissing, and groping my body, mind, and soul. Where was this all headed? I asked myself. But the fog in my consciousness was thick with confusion, doubt, and an inability to cope.

"Don't say anything now. Just think about it. You'll see it's the right thing to do." Carol pulled me to her once more and rubbed the small of my back in a soothing way. I felt comforted by her embrace. Feeling me soften, she moved one hand to my front as she slowly yet firmly rubbed her palm across my breast. My senses were overloaded, and I allowed her to do as she wished. I gave into the sensations and felt urges for her that confused, but also excited me. I knew I was in deep trouble. I also knew I felt powerless to resist her.

"Well, Rick and I thought you two were *never* going to come upstairs again," Gail remarked as she stood from her chair with her brows furrowed and eyebrows raised. Rick kept seated and looked ominous as the smoke from his cigarette shrouded him in a hazy cloud. Too much smoking had a way of giving his skin a lifeless look. He also looked irritated. I couldn't say that I blamed him. It must have seemed strange for Carol and me to disappear downstairs while we left him and Gail alone.

I made sure we said our goodnights quickly so Rick and I could walk the short distance to our house next door. Once inside, Rick repeated his questions of what had happened. I busied myself with changing into my pajamas. I wanted this day to be over.

"Emma, can you tell me what's going on?" I was drawn by how soft Rick had asked me the question. Not antagonistic or accusatory as was his usual approach.

"I don't know, Rick. It just seems like everything is closing in on me. You know, with the move, finding a new rental, and as you know—work is really hectic right now." I was trying to be as honest as I could without being too specific.

Rick held me while we got comfortable in bed. He surprised me by initiating love making for the first time in quite a while. My thoughts were those of guilt since I'd just been held intimately by another just an hour before. It felt good to reconnect with Rick and try to pretend that maybe we were going to be OK, after all. I also dared to dream that this might be the union that would finally get me pregnant.

11

THANKSGIVING DINNER

November 23, 1993, journal entry

I'm so confused. I feel paralyzed in my own life. This whole thing seems way more complicated than I'm able to cope with. I love her. And have feelings of not being able to go on without her. Petrified that I may lose her. But at the same time, I feel dominated by her. She calls me at work all the time now. I try to explain that I have a very fast-paced job where I have little downtime to talk with her on the phone. This seems to make her mad! And she insists how much more important her job is than mine.

After the other night at her house when she told me how attracted she was to me, I finally told her I was unsure of giving up on my marriage yet. I even told her that we were still trying to get pregnant. This made her livid. She acted in a way that was reminiscent of when she found out I have this journal. It's another side of her that really scares me. It seems her pattern is to punish me after she gets mad and that in turn makes me cave in and be sorry. I feel a sense of deprivation when she's withholding. My parents do that, too. In fact, they haven't spoken to me in three years. When I confided in my mom's sister that I'd found and met my birth mother, she immediately told my mom. She betrayed my confidence —I have no idea why she thought that was a good idea. So now my parents are punishing me with their silent treatment. I'm hoping that Carol will get over being mad since we're supposed to be spending Thanksgiving with her and Gail the day after tomorrow. But before that, I have a session with her later today. Man, this is getting so confusing! And the doubt and uncertainty that I feel is growing to the point that I just don't feel I know what I'm doing at all. I get so distracted doing the simplest of things. I miss turns off the freeway, I'm late everywhere I go, I can't eat, and I can't sleep. I'm a mess.

At the top of my to-do list was to find another rental as soon as possible. The extended deadline that Carol had negotiated was fast approaching. I'd purchased the local Laguna paper and started circling all the rentals with a pen. I found only two in Laguna since so many homes had burned. One of the rentals was at the opposite end of town and the other was just a little farther up the hill. Rick and I drove up the short distance to look at the one higher up the hill.

We passed lot after lot of charred remains where Laguna residents used to live. All that was left were half burned palm trees, debris, scorched rubble, and an occasional home that looked amazingly untouched. And in great contrast was an incredible view overlooking the beautiful Pacific Ocean.

Rick looked at me shaking his head side to side, "Why don't we look elsewhere? Outside this warzone. Maybe in Dana Point, or even Laguna Niguel?"

I knew he meant that while the ocean view was fantastic, we would be surrounded by devastation and the endless rebuilding process that would bring noise, construction traffic, and a lot of other inconveniences to consider. Not to mention the possible medical health hazards of living and breathing a toxic environment.

All I could think about was not wanting to move away from being Carol's neighbor. That seemed most pertinent to me.

"I think this rental makes the most sense. It's not too far away. We could pack our cars and move most of our stuff. And the ocean view more than makes up for the decimated neighborhood," I said hopefully.

"Does it?" Rick gave me an exhausted sideway look and then turned away. We were so high on this cliff that we were above the clouds. He lit another cigarette and gazed out from the patio of the rental house at the layer of wispy clouds covering portions of the full-on ocean view below.

I sensed him acquiescing. "I'll start making the arrangements. Set the move date. Call the utilities. The moving van for our furniture. I'll also look into getting us some boxes to start packing." I had moved so often over the last few years that the process was familiar to me. The difficult part for me above all else was the thought of leaving Dr. Carol Brenner—no longer being her next-door neighbor.

Rick, Carol, Gail, and I had planned to meet at the restaurant of a local resort tucked away in one of Laguna's pine and eucalyptus tree-covered canyons for Thanksgiving dinner. I was self-conscious and nervous being seated across the table from Carol and Gail. Did Gail know? Had Carol asked her to move out yet and told her things were over between the two of them? It really didn't appear so. They seemed just as much a couple as ever. This relieved me.

Over the last few days of making moving preparations, actively participating in my life, I had been feeling stronger.

As if my feet were a little more firmly planted on the ground. It was good to see Carol, but I had not been thinking of her non-stop. I was feeling stronger and thankful that the anxiety of finding a rental was now solved. We had signed the mandatory one-year rental agreement—along with paying an excessive security deposit due to Rick's horrendous credit score—just the day before.

Rick seemed excited to be sharing with the table about our impending move. He went on to his next all-time favorite topic—the book he planned to write soon. As I listened and watched Rick charismatically talk and wave his cigarette with expressive gestures, it reminded me that he was a talented showman and storyteller at heart. He had a way of captivating listeners when he wanted to. I recalled at that moment how I had been infatuated with him when we first met for these same reasons.

Carol had seemed especially interested when Rick talked about his writings and started asking questions about her own book she had begun to write.

"Rick, do you think you could look over a few chapters I've written? I'd love to get your feedback," Carol asked my husband. I wasn't sure, but I thought she had batted her eyelashes at him as she asked the favor.

"Well, sure. Go ahead and send it on over." Rick seemed happy to help and more than a little exalted by the attention. I may have been caught by his charisma in the beginning of our relationship, but I was starting to reconcile that Rick was not the mystical guru he professed to be. I had been resistant to acknowledge that he had almost zero follow-through and that the great American novel he was going to write just never seemed to get written. I feared that Rick would take Carol's manuscript and more than likely never return it after sticking it in a drawer somewhere. But in this moment, he was stroking her ego by acting as though they were both artistic writers to be admired and praised.

"So, when's the big *move* day?" Carol's words were calculated and precise. I felt they were intended to confuse and unnerve me. I began to speak, but my mouth went dry and my heart surged as I felt Carol's foot slide up my bare leg underneath the table, concealed by the white tablecloth. I stumbled over my words, sounding just as confused as I felt. What was I to do? What was I to say? But rather than stopping, she continued lightly stroking her bare foot up and down my calf and then up past my knees. My outsides were frozen, but my insides were on fire. I pleaded with Carol with my eyes so she could see I was desperate for her to stop. *Please! Stop!*

The server brought pumpkin pie slices with whipped cream, and I used the opportunity to move my chair back from the table. I pretended I'd dropped something and needed to bend down to pick it up. When I resettled in my chair, I risked a look at Carol who was giving me a coy smile of domination. She looked triumphant that she had flustered me. My panic subsided as I monitored Rick and Gail to see whether they sensed any of what had just transpired. But nothing. It was clear that I was the only one on high alert and feeling both guilt and shame.

12

BLAZING RED FLAGS

November 27, 1993, journal entry

I get so mad at Carol, but I can't seem to stay that way. What she did to me under the table at Thanksgiving dinner was terrible! I was frozen to do anything. But I also must admit that something is really going on. Mostly I just feel so confused. Do I love her in that way? A sexual way? I've never been attracted to another woman before. The truth is, I'm attached to her and feel powerless over whatever is happening. When I think of walking away and not seeing her anymore, it leaves me with feelings of great despair. Like I can't breathe. I haven't felt in control of this situation since the very beginning when I first met Dr. Brenner on my driveway three months ago. Has it really only been three months? I've lost track of time.

I feel guilty thinking negative things about her when all she's done is help me. Loving her feels so essential. It feels like it's all that matters. If I were to lose her, I'm not sure how I could go on. Rick no longer feels like home to me. Dr. Brenner does. I feel as though I have no one else. I've distanced myself from Rick, my parents, my birth mother, and all my friends. I connect as little as possible with the people I work with. No one understands me the way Carol does.

∼

My next session with Dr. Brenner was bizarre. When she brought me into her office, she had a confession.

"Emma, love, I've double-booked appointments today." She said with her eyebrows furrowed and her lips drawn into her mouth. I felt a wave of collapse rising inside me. A panic. Was she going to turn me away and tell me to leave so she could counsel the other booked appointment?

"Oh, I see I've upset you! The worst part is that it looks like I won't be able to fit you in for at least a few days," Dr. Brenner said apologetically, yet with a smile. Already panicked at the thought of not seeing her today, I felt that familiar feeling of deprivation. That well-worn path of not feeling good enough to stick around for. And why was she smiling? Was she happy to see how this was affecting me?

"Listen, I have an idea." Dr. Brenner sounded so upbeat that I immediately looked at her in hopeful anticipation.

"My next patient is only a telephone call. What if you stayed with me while I counseled her on the phone?" Her words hung in the air as I tried to make sense of them. "If you stick around, then I'll be able to have a session with you afterward. Also, there's something I really need to tell you." She used her super-therapist voice. "So, you'll stay?"

Red flag after *red flag*. My critical thinking and sense of autonomy had been so undermined that the opportunity to be with her overshadowed my feelings of respect for myself, as well as for Dr. Brenner's patient to be counseled by phone. I felt a floaty sensation where I felt disconnected from my body. I was in a state of considerable anxiety and indecisiveness.

Dr. Brenner took charge, and seated me in a chair right next to hers. And for the next 50 minutes, I listened and observed her as she counseled someone on the other end of the phone as she stroked my hair and cupped my face in her hands. I was mesmerized by her hypnotic qualities and felt as though I'd been drugged without even knowing it. Watching her only increased my distortion that she must be a goddess that worked magic on those who were lucky enough to be counseled by her.

"Emma, you are so special to me," she said as she hung up the phone from her session. "And *so* beautiful. I just *love* looking at you." I felt as though she wished to devour me at that moment. Maybe this was the same kind of fear Gretel felt when the witch used coercive persuasion to control and captivate her in the German fairytale.

"This is our secret, yeah? No one can know about this. This would probably make me lose my license." For a moment, Dr. Brenner placed her face into her hands as if hiding in shame. Was she crying? And then suddenly she removed her hands and declared, "Now, let's talk about *you*."

I was surprised when she turned her full attention to me. My insides were ignited. Excited that it was time for her to focus on me and I could hopefully feel cared for. It's as if I had merged with her and no longer had my own thoughts anymore. I hadn't even considered how long I'd been gone from work that afternoon. Or how I should be doing some preliminary packing of our house in preparation of the move coming up in a matter of days. All I could concentrate on was my obsession with Dr. Brenner. Nothing else mattered. I felt I had indeed given her total control.

But it suddenly became clear she was not going to make me her priority. Instead, as we sat close together in the circular bucket chairs in her office, Dr. Brenner leaned forward with her eyes sparkling and a smile showing her perfect white teeth—and placed her hands on my knees, squeezing gently as she exclaimed, *"I've kicked Gail out!"*

≈

I experienced another trance-like state hearing Dr. Brenner's words. She had told Gail to leave the home they owned together and that their relationship of being a committed couple of eight years was over. I left her office in a state of profound confusion. And—total fear. Carol hadn't stopped with only telling me of her new single status. She went on to share with me her comprehensive plan for *us* to become a couple.

I had felt a mixture of nausea and ecstasy at hearing the news. Dr. Brenner was professing her love for me. It felt so good to be held by her. Wanted by her. So why was I experiencing feelings of personal disintegration? The pain to my psyche was severe. I didn't know if I was ready to leave Rick or not. Being a couple with Dr. Brenner felt more like a fantasy than a real possibility. What did that even mean? I didn't know what I was feeling about anything. I wished I had someone else to talk with. Someone impartial. But there was no one.

Later that night at home, I was in a fog—more than usual after a session with Dr. Brenner. I didn't trust myself to say too much to Rick—especially about Carol and Gail splitting up. The thick, dark fog in my mind, body, and soul consisted of utter confusion and the preoccupation of thinking of nothing but her. Carol and me together. Carol holding me. And did I dare think or even consider a life with Carol? The thought made my brain feel as though it were blowing fuses. Contrarily, the idea of being without her seemed tethered to my very survival. My psyche felt as though it were splitting in two.

Rick came in looking somber and sat at the kitchen table. Grabbing and lighting another cigarette, he waited to say something until he had it fully lit. He leaned back in his chair, took a full drag and then slowly exhaled the smoke in a controlled plume.

"I guess you heard about Carol and Gail splitting." Rick stared at me. "I talked with Gail out front after work. She's pretty upset."

"It sounded like it'd been coming on for a while," I added.

"Gail told me Carol gave her no warning and just said to pack her things and leave. She said that she'd met someone else." Rick took another puff on his close to finished Marlboro.

I was getting used to living in a state of fight or flight— just as I had in my childhood home. Chaos was the norm. And if there wasn't any drama, someone in my household would be sure to create something. I had somehow recreated that similar constant turmoil in my adult life.

"Are you ready for the move, Emma?" Rick said as he stubbed out his cigarette and reached into his shirt pocket for another. "You've barely packed a box."

"I've just had so much going on. I'll start tonight." It was like I was living a double life. One foot in one life, one in another. Living in liminal space. Not fully being in either one. And then it struck me—the similarity of my life at present and having been relinquished at birth and then being adopted. I'd always felt as though I'd been purchased by my adoptive parents to fulfill a role as their dutiful daughter. I was never allowed or encouraged to be my true self. I felt like an imposter even to myself. And even though I'd searched and found my birth mother, there was no long-lost connection there, either. Where did I fit? My birth mother had looked at me with pleading eyes to take care of her and be her key to understanding herself. I couldn't do that. Only she could have done that. I quit trying.

"Emma," Rick spoke. And then stopped. "Emma, she's manipulating you."

"Who is?" I knew who he meant. I didn't want to hear it.

"You know *who*," Rick spat. "Did you know she's done this to other patients before? Someone named Maria. Gail told me all about it. Brenner had an affair with her, and she was her patient. That's a serious breach in her code of ethics. Don't be stupid, Emma!"

"*So!* That doesn't have anything to do with me! Please just leave me alone and let me start packing." I had learned from my parents how to shut down a conversation and use my anger as justification to walk away from an unwanted, uncomfortable conversation. I was thinking how it was just like Rick to want to deprive me of someone loving me. Five years earlier, he had effectively isolated me from my family, friends, and kept me from developing any interests that did not put him in the center of things. Now he was trying to poison me against Carol. Someone who truly cared about me and was actively trying to help me. She also found me attractive. Sexy. Rick could only talk and write poetry of his past loves as desirable and exquisitely beautiful. But he seemed unable to think of me in that way. At least not anymore. He'd been ignoring me for years, especially sexually—and now he was jealous of Carol for taking an interest in me.

13

GRETEL'S IN THE FIRE

December 3, 1993, journal entry

Tomorrow the movers come. Rick and I are to move farther up the hill to a rental that's surrounded by the charred and seared remains of what used to be a neighborhood. I have never felt so off balance in my life. I feel both Rick and Carol tugging on my sanity. Neither will be happy until I split into two.

W hen I got to my office that day, my desk phone's voicemail light was flashing red. I immediately felt anger. It was 9:30 a.m. and Carol had already left three messages. One was to ask me how I was feeling. The second one was demanding I call her as soon as possible. And the third was asking why I hadn't called her back yet. She sounded not at all like the super-therapist I idolized, but more like a desperate person trying to control another. It didn't sit well with me that day since I'd gotten little sleep, I was in a fight with Rick, and I'd not eaten anything since the day before. Being at work was pointless because I was far beyond being productive.

As I sat at my desk doing close to nothing, I found myself wondering how I'd gotten so dependent upon another person. First it had been dependence on Rick to be my savior, now it had become Dr. Brenner. It was making me mad at myself for getting so deeply, emotionally mixed up with my therapist. Then I remembered poor Maria who had supposedly had an affair with Dr. Brenner. Carol would call her "crazy Maria." That seemed a grossly uncaring way to describe a past patient who was to be in your care. I looked down at the mess on my desk. I couldn't make sense of the many papers I was supposed to be reading, memos I was supposed to be writing, calls I was supposed to be making, meetings I was expected to attend. My ability to concentrate felt like walking through mush. I heard a phone ringing and realized it was my own.

"Hi, this is Emma." I expected to hear someone from our media department, or maybe someone from the creative team. But it was Dr. Brenner.

"Why haven't you called me, Emma? I've been worried." She sounded genuinely concerned. She sounded like super-therapist, Dr. Brenner.

"I'm sorry, I just got to work not too long ago," I said. The reality was I was having a difficult time even using words to talk with her on the phone. It's like my brain had been seized and I had been transported into a thick fog.

"Have you not even listened to the messages I sent you? This is of great importance. I need you to listen, Emma … Emma? I need you to come and see me as soon as you can. Do you think you can drive safely to my house?" Her remarks helped to clear my head a little. It sounded as though she knew how messed up I was.

"Um … yeah, I guess. I'm not getting any work done here

anyway. I don't feel so great. My head really hurts." I confessed.

"It's all going to be OK, Emma. That's what my messages were about. I've taken care of *everything*. I've done what I knew you weren't strong enough to do. So, I did it for you." Her voice was so soothing. I wasn't sure what she was talking about, but she made it sound comforting.

"What's *everything*? I don't understand." An anxiety started creeping over me. Suddenly I had the feeling that everything was about to change.

"You don't have to worry about the move with Rick anymore," Dr. Brenner explained in an eerily even tone.

"I've moved all your belongings next door. You'll live with *me* now. I love you so much!"

I placed my head on my desk and cried.

I slowly drove on the freeway to Carol's house in Laguna. It was Friday. She was off on Fridays. She greeted me at the door and led me down to her bedroom where she laid me down and I curled up into a ball on top of her comforter. I cried and remained tucked in a ball as tight as I could. All I felt was impending doom. I had a deficit of language to describe the severity of what I was feeling.

"Here, Emma. Drink this." Carol handed me a scotch and water. It tasted of mainly scotch. And that was OK by me. The more the fire, the better I felt. She gave me another as I began to unfurl from the fetal position I'd been in. I noticed she was drinking more than a few, too.

"How did you even get inside my house to take my stuff?" I was looking at her for the first time since I'd arrived. The alcohol had sedated me.

"Remember I fed your cats one weekend while you and

Rick were away? I never gave you back your key." Carol sat next to me on the bed.

The thought of sitting casually on Carol's bed, Dr. Brenner's bed, in her home, which she said was now my home—further destabilized me. The floaty feeling returned, now mixed with the warm embracing effects of alcohol. What the absolute hell was I doing?! What was Rick thinking about all this? Did he even know yet? How could I be allowing this to happen? So many questions were like loud thunder inside my head, haunting me and bringing me to the brink of feeling insane.

"It's going to be OK, Emma." Carol kept repeating this phrase as though it would make it true. I became aware of her hands on my arms, in my hair, and pulling me closer to her. The alcohol had smoothed out my emotions where I accepted her touching, stroking, and then kissing me. I fell into a kind of drunken abyss, giving over all my power and unable to reject being dominated and controlled.

I awakened that next morning in a bed that was not my own and felt as if I were caught in a deadly spider web complete with a scotch hangover. I had the explicit thought that all those red flags I'd been whooshing away were trying to tell me that *a fire was coming*. A deadly all-consuming fire. Dr. Carol Brenner was that fire. And now I was burning inside the witch's oven.

My next thoughts were of Rick. I hadn't even called him yesterday, or last night. Today, he would be moving by himself to the charred neighborhood up the hill. I wouldn't be helping him. Or moving with him. I wouldn't have my cats. What was I doing?

"Are you awake, Emma?" I pretended to be asleep. "I'll be

in the kitchen when you're ready to get up. I'll make us some breakfast and coffee." I couldn't deny this sounded good. When had I last eaten? I couldn't have gotten more than a few hours of sleep. A fitful kind of sleep. Sleep that was full of anxiety dreams where I'm trying to figure something out, but the answers eluded me. I'd woken myself up at one point talking out in my sleep. I felt like total hell. Emotionally, physically, spiritually.

The smell of the coffee convinced me to get up, take some aspirin, brush my teeth, and grab my robe she'd placed out for me at the foot of her bed. She had brought *all* my clothes from my house and had given me my own walk-in closet. I headed upstairs to Carol's kitchen. Her home was lovely. Very creatively decorated. It looked expensive. I took a seat in one of the Italian-styled wrought iron barstools and leaned my elbows onto the brown and cream-colored granite countertop. The cold countertop felt wonderful against my hot skin. My head was still throbbing but a couple of sips of the hot coffee did wonders. As I began to focus on my surroundings, I looked out through the bay window straight ahead and saw the beautiful blue Pacific Ocean. The view was stunning. However, my focus remained on trying to physically feel better.

"Are you feeling OK?" Carol asked softly. She gently laid her hand on my shoulder as she placed a plate with a just cooked omelet in front of me and a side of fresh cut fruit. I stared at my plate. The heat from her hand that remained on my shoulder, radiated. Like a transfer of energy. I began to cry. A big heaving cry.

"I know this is hard. Let go of your resistance, Emma. Everything will be so much clearer for you when you reach acceptance." Dr. Brenner was holding me like a mother would her beloved child. I melted into her. I wanted to believe her.

"You must try harder. This is difficult for me, too. Did you think about that?" Carol suddenly pulled back, her eyes red from last night's scotch. "Do you see how you're making this *all about you?*"

I felt immediate shame. "What? Wait! No! I'm sorry. I think about you all the time. I'm so preoccupied with thinking about you that I'm making myself sick!" Those words were true.

"If that were true—then you'd be acting a little more grateful. I pulled you out of a dead-end relationship with Rick. He doesn't *care* about you! And neither do your parents, or that woman you call your birth mother."

The person holding me like a loving mother suddenly became, without warning, an angry and scary version of Dr. Brenner. I'd seen this version of her only a few other times—and would whoosh it away as soon as the super-therapist Dr. Brenner would return. This felt just like when my adoptive mother would send me the implicit and explicit messages that she found me unlovable and didn't think I was significant enough to nurture. Yet I was expected to remain eternally grateful to her. She had not solved her own childhood trauma and would often take out her sense of inadequacies on others. Especially my older brother and me. As a child needing to survive, I learned to acquiesce—whatever the circumstances—to get back into her good graces.

"Well, OK then. Good. I don't want to hear anything more about him. Can I get you another cup of coffee?" Carol said cheerfully as she grabbed my cup to pour me another.

"Hey, I know, let's just get out of town for a few days. Get a change of scenery. Maybe go up to the mountains?" Carol was planning our trip before I even had a chance to put my coffee cup down. I was frozen and didn't trust myself to speak out for fear she might change personas again.

"Remember you talked about trading your car in to get an

SUV? Wouldn't that be perfect for traveling in the mountains? I have a patient named Paul who's a car salesman at the Ford dealership. Why don't you go get dressed and we'll head on over there!" Carol hopped off her barstool next to me and started busily cleaning her kitchen.

I sat there frozen. Head still aching. My skin still feeling the sickness that hangovers wrap you up in. And trying to make sense of what had transpired in the matter of moments. I couldn't afford to buy a new car. I had *talked* about *wanting* a new car, but that didn't mean I was ready to buy one! And who was this Paul? Was this yet another inappropriate therapist/patient relationship? Had she also asked him to keep their relationship on the downlow? And, in the periphery of my thoughts, was her admission of seeing yet another patient outside the confines of her office. I was pretty sure that was against some kind of therapeutic rule.

"Carol, I don't think I can afford to buy a car today." I stared at her hoping this wouldn't set her off again. Hmm, walking on eggshells—such a familiar scenario from my childhood of growing up with emotionally immature parents.

"Paul will give you an excellent deal! He owes me a favor, anyway. With your trade-in, you may not have to put down any additional money!" Carol approached me and wrapped me up into her familiar loving embrace. Her hugs always produced in me a sense that my heart was glowing and radiating. It felt intoxicating.

What kind of favor did her patient, Paul, owe her?

14

THE MASK WAS SLIPPING

December 11, 1993, journal entry

Carol kept me up most of the night talking about how beautiful she thinks I am and how much she loves me. It's overwhelming. All the emotion. I begged her to let me sleep. But anytime I'd start to shut my eyes, she'd start kissing me again. I can't deny I feel wonderful when she holds me. But I'm unsure if I'm sexually attracted to her. She's been telling me that I'm resisting being able to admit that I'm a lesbian. I'm so confused why I feel attracted to her but also feel as if she's the mother I never had. What's that about?

Five hours later, Carol and I were in my newly purchased navy blue Ford Bronco driving northeast toward Big Bear in the San Bernardino National Forest. Carol had been wrong about me not needing to put additional funds toward buying the car. I found myself signing a monthly lease agreement that was well out of my budget. It all happened so fast. I ignored the red-hot turmoil in my gut and signed the papers. Carol was by my side the entire time. Holding my hand. Patting my back. Several times she kissed me seductively. It was as if she wanted her patient, Paul, who was our sales associate, to know she was claiming ownership of me. That we were a couple. That made my skin prickle.

The two-and-a-half-hour drive from the coast was not especially scenic until getting close to the foot of the mountains. Then began the altitude climb with the twisting winding road lined with towering pines. California State Route 18, or the Rim of the World Scenic Byway, is 110 miles through the San Bernardino National Forest, nicknamed for its stunning views along the cliffs of the San Bernardino Mountains.

With slopes rising steeply on both sides and the road hugging rugged cliffs as we traversed a series of curves, I pulled over and allowed Carol to take the wheel. My brow was covered in beads of sweat and I was perspiring through my clothes. I was starting to feel panic not only because of the stressful drive, but because of how it seemed that the treacherous drive mimicked my present situation. My continued sleeplessness and lack of eating were contributing to my cloudy, floaty, indecisive, lack of critical thinking abilities. And even still, my desperate attachment to Dr. Carol Brenner remained. And it continued to overrule any red flags of behavior or clarity in which to see the situation clearly. It's as though I went freely into the belly of the beast, or that I was Gretel blindly walking into the witch's oven. The beauty, heat, and perceived love promised by the fire—who was Dr. Brenner—drew me in and twisted, churned, and turned me in on myself. It was excruciatingly painful. And I had the sickening sense that there was no escape.

"Emma," Carol began at dinner later that night, "I've decided to not charge you for our therapy sessions any longer." We were at a dimly lit, expensive Italian restaurant with the charm of a well-appointed cottage nestled in the alpine scenery. Her statement struck me as odd. Were we still doing therapy?

"Since we're a couple now, we'll no longer do *traditional* therapy—since that would be unethical. But don't worry! I'll still give you therapy!" Carol covered my hands that were resting on the table with her own. Her touch was warm. It made my emotions stir. The drug-like effect her touch had on me seemed to override my usual sensibilities.

Carol leaned in close. "Tell me more about your rich parents. Sounds like they do well since they own expensive homes in Aspen, Colorado and in your hometown. I'm always looking for investors for my projects. Maybe you could set me up a meeting with them?"

What?! I was screaming inside my head. I pulled back from her touch, as if to break the spell and retorted, "My parents and I aren't even speaking right now! And you've been encouraging me to break *all* communication with them. Now you're saying you want me to set up a meeting with them so you can ask for money?" I had found my voice at that moment. But only for a second—because Dr. Brenner retaliated with words that were meant to scorch, singe, and sear.

Her facial features began to contort and resemble my mother's face when she'd become angry at me. Eyes squinting and pinched together at the interior corners. Forehead and eyebrows lifted and wrinkled. Nostrils flared and nose scrunched as if she were smelling something bad. Lips pursed and ready to spew words meant to intimidate and strip me of my self-worth. My senses were on high alert.

"I *knew you needed to get on medication for your disorder.* You're so far out of touch with reality!" She shook her head so vigorously back and forth that a little spittle started forming at the corners of her mouth. "I see *all my efforts* have been wasted on you. I thought you were a person of substance—but you've been out for *yourself* all along."

Fear of losing connection with her punched me in the gut. I regretted my words the moment they left my mouth. Guilt and shame settled upon me. I was selfish. I was ungrateful. I panicked to make things right again. This was my "flight" response after almost fighting back.

"I'm *all* you have now, Emma! Have you thought about that?" Carol hissed. My body shaking and sweating, I watched her get up and walk out of the restaurant. A familiar feeling in the pit of my stomach began. Deprivation. Abandonment. Not being good enough to stay for. The feeling of not being significant enough to be listened to and seen. I'd do anything to get her back. I couldn't think of anything but that.

The next weeks living with Dr. Brenner as a couple were a blur. My inner compass was spinning over my loss of self. It was a feeling of madness. I was often unable to go to work. Unable to focus. And feeling as though I was unable to continue staying with her, yet unable to leave her. The physical and psychological attachment I had with her seemed to be, to some degree, related to the thwarted attachment process from my birth. During the birthing process, the critical oxytocin hormone is released into the bloodstream which promotes mother and child bonding. I now understand that the feeling that's in every cell of my body and psyche is my "primal wound." The primal wound is there because I lost my first mother and my entire first family at birth, and then was adopted into another family, forever altering the trajectory of my life and my sense of self. It's a trauma that has repeated itself throughout my life. Some experts in the field of psychology even say it's a complex developmental trauma that changes adoptees neurologically. In psychotherapist Nathaniel Branden's book, *Six Pillars of Self-Esteem*, he says, "the greater a child's terror, and the earlier it is experienced, the harder it becomes to develop a strong and healthy sense of self." During the painstaking search for my birth parents I'd conducted a few years earlier, I had read the clinical notes describing me as an infant. I was "a sober baby, one who didn't cry, didn't smile or engage, and one who had difficulty eating." This sounds like an infant in shock to me—proving the stress I had endured from relinquishment.

When my first mother relinquished me, and then handed me to strangers who adopted me, my attachment phase with my biological mother never occurred. It left me unattached, untethered, and oxytocin deprived. It was also one of the main reasons I became vulnerable to a predator like Dr. Brenner who, even without my primal wound, was actively searching for her next victim. Having been raised by narcissistic adoptive parents, I was even more susceptible to this exploitative, cultic, egocentric therapist.

A few weeks after Dr. Brenner had moved my belongings into her home, I reached out to Rick. It grounded me to talk with him and to hear that our cats were adjusting to the new rental house where he'd moved. All by himself. Without me.

"Emma, don't you see what she's doing? She's manipulating you. She's way beyond being unethical. I've bought a reference book I'd like you to see if you're willing. It's all about therapist/patient exploitation. It's exactly what she's done to you! Can't you see that?!" Rick seemed patient yet urgent in wanting to get through to me. It had been good to connect with him, but it was probably too much, too soon for him to try to educate me about Dr. Brenner. Inside my head all I heard was, *"But she said she loves me! And she said that you are the enemy."*

"It says right here that an unethical therapist will try to strip your defenses down to the point of placing you in a childlike state—it's so they can more easily manipulate you for their own self-interest," Rick said and then paused. I listened. I couldn't help but reflect on the fact that Rick's manipulations and how he'd tried isolating me during our marriage wasn't too very different from this.

Rick continued: "Cultic relationships, according to International Cultic Studies Association (ICSA), the 1985 definition of a cult, or in this case, a one-on-one cult, is 'a group, movement, or single person exhibiting great or excessive devotion or dedication to some person, idea, or thing and employing unethical, manipulative, or coercive techniques of persuasion and control. For example: Isolation from former friends and family; debilitation; use of special methods to heighten suggestibility and subservience; powerful group pressures; information management; suspension of individuality or critical judgment; promotion of total dependency on the leader and fear of leaving. These techniques are designed to advance the goals of the leader to the actual or possible detriment of the individual, group, their families, or the community.'"

I felt a kind of mental paralysis when hearing this definition and went into shutdown mode. I couldn't process what Rick was saying.

"So … you're saying I've been duped?!" I was agitated and ready to end the phone call.

"Emma, it happens all the time. More than you'd think. It's not your fault! She used your vulnerabilities against you. And she fooled me, Gail, and who knows how many others! *Remember Maria?!"*

Rick was sounding compassionate but it also sounded as

though he was jealous and disbelieving that I'd picked Carol over him. However, he was acting much more like the charismatic Rick I'd met five years earlier who actively pursued me by acting loving and caring. He even said, "Emma, It's OK if you leave me but I can't let you end up with her. She's not who she says she is."

Hearing his words made my heart soften a little until it made me mad that it took someone literally stealing his wife away before he wanted to start treating me right. And if anyone wasn't who they portrayed themselves to be, it was Rick! He had promised me he was an enlightened, creative person who craved a life of truth and beauty. But what I'd discovered over the last five years of being with him was that Rick was a chronic procrastinator riddled with inauthenticity. I couldn't take any more of Rick's words against Dr. Brenner. I hung up the phone, but his voice was still loud and clear in my head.

"You were bound by undue influence ... Enveloped by a powerful combination of forces that were in many instances authoritarian, totalistic, manipulative and harmful ... Have you ever heard of Stockholm Syndrome? Loving your captor?"

Moments later I received a short email from Rick.

"Emma,

Just tell me this—has she started having you do her personal errands or ordering you to take care of her house— in other words—basically making your life revolve around hers? Emma, she used coercive persuasion to get you to *buy a new car!* The book says that all these things are the trademark of a person with narcissistic personality disorder, or even a sociopath. Please just think about it.

Love,
     Rick"

15
EYES OF THE BEAST

January 8, 1994, journal entry

Carol brought up my journal again. She was insistent. She made me read it to her. I was embarrassed since I hadn't planned on anyone ever reading my private thoughts. Especially not her! She admonished me again about how I can never go to the board of ethics and tell of our relationship. She reminded me how this relationship was all my idea in the first place. I was unsure about that since she's the one who moved my personal belongings from my house to hers for me to live with her. I didn't say anything.

My brain was sizzling as if it'd been placed in a hot pan with oil. Dr. Brenner had been asking more and more of me—insisting her job was of more importance than mine. She wanted me to make sure dinner was planned, to take her dogs to the vet, her clothes to the cleaners. The demands weren't placed all at once. She'd been asking and adding on a little at a time. And it was the manner of how she'd ask now, instead of the way she did in the beginning. When she'd gently take my hands, look deeply into my eyes, and make her demands softly. But suddenly, I started seeing more and more of Dr. Brenner's persona that frightened me and reminded me of my mother. She could turn into a monster in a split second. The super-therapist was gone. The charismatic goddess gone. The seductress gone. Her well affixed mask used consistently in the beginning was beginning to slip.

One day, I arrived home from work before Carol and started feeding her dogs. I had been instructed to do so when she called me at work checking up on me the way she'd been doing ever since she'd moved me in with her.

"I don't like that you work at the same place as Rick. You should get a different job—or better yet, quit work all together and just manage my home. You know I have such a beautiful oceanfront beach house—anyone should be so lucky, right?!"

I had now lived with Carol for about a month and was starting to give her more and more pushback when I'd feel her trying to oppress and control me. I also couldn't deny that some of the things Rick had been sending me to read about exploitative therapists and how they manipulate and control their victims was starting to look and sound very familiar.

"Why would I quit my job? I have a new car payment each month, remember? And anyway, I need to talk to Rick about our cats and how I've been gone for a month now." I let my voice trail off knowing that I was about to see Dr. Brenner's version of Dr. Jekyll and Mr. Hyde come into play again.

"What do you mean you've been talking to *Rick?!* Oh my God, you've got to be fucking kidding me?! He doesn't love you! He's weak and doesn't even find you sexually appealing. You told me he rarely makes love to you!"

My throat constricted letting no words come out. Carol's words were harsh, but not without truth. I had confessed these intimate details about Rick's and my sex life during our therapy sessions. Now it seemed she was using my words against me. In that moment, I reflected on how a charismatic, narcissistic person's spiel often contains portions of truth, which is how the psychological hook is set. Just then, Dr. Brenner, the super-therapist, came back online.

"Oh, Emma, love, you *know* I love you. *I'm* the one who can comfort you. Let's do a therapy session when I get home in a while. After you feed the dogs, OK?"

I stood waiting for Carol to come home that day while I gazed out over the ocean from her outdoor deck. Glancing to my left, I could see the corner of my old deck from where I used to live next door. My thoughts were inundated by the irony of how many times I'd stood on that deck yearning to talk and be close with Dr. Brenner before she moved me in with her. Now that I was basically her possession, I was unsure of my wishes anymore.

The sun was setting into a thin layer of clouds, ablaze with orange and red rays shining up into the fading blue sky. So peaceful. The movement and sounds of the ocean soothed my tortured thoughts and feelings of being a stranger in a strange land. But … how Laguna calls to me. It's always seemed to whisper "home" like no place ever has. Mother ocean was saying, "Run, dear one. Things are not as they seem." Little cracks of light were starting to seep into my awareness. The thought of water putting out fire trickled into my consciousness. My denial was a little less ironclad and allowed certain truths to be illuminated. One of Rick's recent emails referred to the tactics used by cult leaders, sociopaths, and narcissistic types "to enthrall" a victim. Rick wrote, "To enthrall is to enslave. It's a type of spiritual rape. Mystical sense of rapture. Passionate emotional devotion to a leader is expected." He went on to say, "Thralldom is a form of bondage. Slavery. Servitude."

Carol's dogs and I were jolted by the sudden noisy, vibrating sound of the garage door opening. Then I felt in my gut the reverberant closing of the door leading from the garage into the kitchen. She was home. What followed was the slow, steady clicking of her black slingback pumps across the terracotta tiled floor. I looked over my shoulder from where I was standing on the deck and locked eyes with Dr. Brenner. An icy chill shot through my insides. She looked at me as if she knew I was having glimmers of clarity about my situation. I suddenly felt like a prisoner who needed to shield my true thoughts. What were my thoughts? Still unsure, and far from deciding to leave her, I relied on my fawn response. Acquiesce. Don't let her see what I'm truly thinking and feeling. Stay safe.

And where would I go if I should leave? These thoughts haunted me. Back to Rick? But we had so many serious unresolved issues. Strike out on my own? I overwhelmed myself with these decisions that seemed too daunting to think about.

Dr. Brenner was then fully facing me in a posture of power. Backlight by the soft kitchen lights, she looked every bit the confident super-therapist/goddess I'd built her up to be. She was polished and stylish in her business suit dress, gold jewelry and black pumps. And, of course, those intimidating designer black-rimmed eyeglasses. A very long silence ensued. She opened her arms and invited me to step forward to embrace her. I complied. I felt an immediate fire ignite within me as I fell into her arms. She was like a dangerous magnet I couldn't resist.

In my trance-like state, Dr. Brenner effortlessly maneuvered me to the closest unobstructed wall. I was thinking, what was it with her and the technique of placing me up against a wall? It seemed to be an act of dominance, submission, and seduction. And it definitely was for me at that moment. She pressed her body forcibly against mine as I could feel the heat of her breath against my ear. Against my neck. I was being dominated. I felt powerless to do anything but stand in the fire.

Dr. Brenner suddenly broke away from me, excitedly exclaiming, "Can you guess who called me today?" I just stared wide-eyed waiting for her to tell me.

"Crazy Maria! She went on and on about how much she loves and misses me. She is *so* obsessed! It's really a shame she's so unstable because she's quite *exquisite*."

I stared at Dr. Brenner with her authoritative-looking glasses right up in my face. My thoughts were—it sounds as though she wants to make me jealous. I started getting curious about Maria. How long ago did this happen?

"What happened between you and Maria?" I asked.

"She was a patient of mine—but I stopped therapy with her the moment we began the affair." Dr. Brenner seemed to be trying to justify the course of events. I'd learned recently through Rick that even if she had stopped treating Maria the moment they became sexual, she still violated the professional code of ethics that she took an oath to uphold. If found guilty, her license would be revoked.

Carol continued, "She was too unstable, and I told her I couldn't see her anymore. When she started threatening to kill herself, I really had to distance myself. I couldn't have her talking to the board and getting my license revoked. Luckily, she was never strong enough to do that," Dr. Brenner said with an ugly chuckle.

"What if she had gone through with it?" I asked.

"With what?" Carol asked defensively.

"What if she had actually killed herself? You were her doctor. Weren't you supposed to help her instead of having an affair with her? Wouldn't you have felt responsible *for her death?!*" I felt the room tilt. No air—just fear. Dr. Brenner began changing in front of my eyes.

This time she slammed me against the wall with such force that it made me gasp and almost simultaneously expel all the air from my lungs. My mind and body were in shock as I stared at her in fear and disbelief. The whites of her eyes had reddened and beads of sweat were forming on her upper lip. I felt as though I was suddenly looking into the eyes of a beast. The last female who had ever shoved me and been physically violent towards me was my mother. When I didn't act or respond the way she'd want me to, or she felt like taking her own inadequacies out on me, my mother had never refrained from hitting me hard, and hitting me often. I endured many years of having to allow my mother to abuse me physically and psychologically. Until one day, when I was seventeen years old. She hit me for the very last time. I looked into the eyes of a dark soul, who was my mother, and finally found my voice. With my own arm raised coura-geously above my head, I spoke the words, *"Don't you EVER hit me again!"* It was as if the searing last slaps of my mother had broken the rage I'd suppressed throughout childhood. My fury replaced my silence. Fury at her for the abuse; and fury towards myself for letting her get away with it for so long. It felt hot. It felt consuming. And it erupted.

My eyes didn't leave Dr. Brenner's. Eyes of a dark soul similar to my mother's.

That was the moment I knew I would plan my escape.

Then it was *me* sucking up all the energy in the room. Sweet clarity had finally come to pay me a visit. It would turn out to be a *short* visit, but I knew it was going to be enough to give me the burst of strength needed to escape my oppressor. If only poor Maria had been stronger. If she had an advocate like I had with Rick who was still sending me emails full of information to educate me of the harsh realities of narcissistic therapists who exploit their patients. And how the imbalance of power can result in a cultic one-on-one abusive relationship. I never knew these things. I didn't even know I had the right to interview a therapist first before accepting them as my counselor. I had unknowingly given her all my power. Right from the start.

"Well, well." Carol began as she slowly stepped away and released me from her grip. "Remember one thing, my dear. And let me be very, very clear. You should remember who I am—and why you *should never, ever, fuck with me.*"

THE ESCAPE

I didn't sleep the last night I lived with my psychologist, Dr. Carol Brenner. When she placed her hand on me during the night, I feigned sleep. My heartbeat was pounding thunderously—it was all I could hear in my head and feel pulsating throughout my body. I was certain she could hear it, too. As I lay there motionless, hour after hour, I was planning my escape. Mentally going through each step of exactly how I was going to cut free from her grasp. I had already resigned myself to going back to Rick and my marriage. While it didn't feel completely right, it *was* a solution to escape my captor. Rick had been—and still was—supportive in trying to help me deprogram from all the levels of entanglement and ensnarement that Dr. Brenner had bound me so tightly in. I would come to learn later how long and arduous a road I truly had to go until being totally free from her.

Carol's alarm woke me at 6:00 a.m. so I must have dozed off at some point. Nonetheless, it took me no time to fully awaken to mobilize and begin to execute my plan. I found myself to be the most clear-headed I'd felt in months. It was like the madness and instability I'd been feeling since meeting her had momentarily lifted. I dressed and met her at the breakfast table, and we shared coffee. I tried very hard to not look at her. She always looked so polished, and her appearance seemed to feed into my distortion of who she truly was. It was imperative that I begin to demystify the supposed "guru" that I had been thinking her to be. And those doctor eyeglasses—those I for sure couldn't stare into for very long without feeling intimidated.

"You're not very talkative this morning. Hmm, what's up?" She said lowering her head to give me a penetrating stare over the top of her glasses. "If you're still thinking about *'poor Maria'*—don't. *I'm* the one who suffered. Ha! It's just like her to try getting all the sympathy."

"I'm fine. Just trying to wake up," I said as I hid my face, pretending to be shaking off a night's sleep.

"Oh, OK then. I'm going to have to dash. I have an early morning patient. I've left a to-do list for you by the phone to get done today. You'll be a love and clean up the kitchen, too, won't you?" Carol said as she jumped off her kitchen barstool and headed for the door with her car keys. "I'll call you later. Come here, give me a hug and kiss."

It was the first time I had cringed at the thought of being touched or kissed by her. I tried hard to fake the hug. She was in such a hurry, she didn't seem to notice her touch hadn't given me the usual thrilling electrical charge it had in the past. I was relieved.

I didn't dare breathe until I felt the vibration of the garage door closing and then coming to an abrupt stop. Just to make sure she was gone, I looked out the window and caught sight of her black Infinity moving farther and farther away, down the steep winding hill to the town below. I immediately set my escape plan into full motion. First, I called in sick to work—*again*. I had missed so much work over the last six months since being involved with Dr. Brenner that it was unfathomable I hadn't been terminated. Looking to the side of the home phone, there were approximately ten items on Carol's to-do list was on the counter next to the phone. She fully expected me to complete her tasks that day:

1. Feed the dogs/Remember only half a cup/Only one treat apiece
2. Take the dogs to the groomer/Give them exact grooming instructions/Make sure they get matching bows/Pick them up before 5:00 p.m./Feed them again at 6:00
3. Pick up cleaning from the cleaners
4. Let carpet workers into the house on your lunch break/They don't need to know that the carpet wasn't damaged due to the fire. I've claimed the damage on my insurance as being "fire damage" related so they'll pay for me to get all new carpet downstairs!
5. Get mail/Go to post office to pick up package
6. Start laundry/Delicates to be hand washed
7. Make golf tee time for 18 holes this Saturday
8. Make bed and clean up kitchen/Make sure countertops are wiped well
9. Pick up my watch from jewelers/Set time ten minutes fast
10. Pick up dinner: two lasagnas from Romano's by 5:45/Make sure salad has one-part romaine, and three-parts mixed lettuce (endive, arugula, and red leaf) DON'T FORGET THE GARLIC BREAD like last time!!!

Just then the phone rang. I jumped, letting out a loud soprano-like scream. My body instantly went rigid and my heart pounded furiously. Since childhood, I've had an overdeveloped startle response. This was from my parent's angry outbursts and use of physical force when expressing themselves. Momentarily confused about whether to answer or not, I stood paralyzed in Dr. Brenner's kitchen with her dogs staring up at me expectantly.

"Hello?"

"Hi, love. I just wanted to remind you that I love you and if you want a child, I'm more than willing to make sure we get a baby," Carol informed me.

"What?!" I was unsure of where this was coming from. I panicked thinking she must be paranoid that I'm leaving and going back to Rick. So suspicious that she wanted me to know we could raise a child together, too. I must have hesitated too long because her persona changed instantly.

"Emma ... what ... are ... you ... up ... to!?" Dr. Brenner said in a long, low hissing growl.

My blood ran cold with a chilling feeling that she was watching and monitoring my every move. I knew she wouldn't be home until the end of the day but everything in my body was telling me to pack my things and get the hell out as quickly as possible.

"Nothing! What do you mean? I've got to go. I'm going to be late for work!" My emotions were a mix of fear and anger fueled by adrenaline. I hung up the phone without answering her. I was in a panic now. My entire body felt engulfed in flames. When did everything take such a drastic turn with Dr. Brenner? It was as if her well-appointed mask had come crashing to the floor. And the weight of all the red flags I'd ignored had finally caused the shelf to collapse. Somehow, she had actively disconnected and dismantled my intuition. And I was watching it all in horror. I ran downstairs and frantically began gathering all my things and shoving them into my new Bronco SUV. Memories of her harsh words from the night before about her ex-patient and lover, Maria, both sickened and infuriated me. Was Maria even still alive? And if so, in what condition? It was obvious by Carol's words she did not care.

More than anything, Dr. Brenner's behavior had chilled and frightened me enough to trigger a childhood memory of my own mother. I had opened a sliding door late one night that led from my bedroom into another room to find my mother standing motionless in the dark just inches from my face with cigarette smoke swirling up and around her pale, contorted face. Her cigarette glowed red at its tip. She had been eavesdropping on the other line while I was on the phone with my boyfriend, who she was trying to prevent me from having a relationship with. Standing there shaking in the dark, I felt a sudden hard sharp blow to my right cheek. An immediate stinging, pulsating pain rose from my face, and my right eye protectively closed from where the slap had partially landed. A pang ripped through me, deep and jagged like something sawing at my insides. The panic and fear fueled me to run back to my room, open my bedroom window, kick out the screen, and sprint into the night. I ended up two miles away at a friend's house in the middle of the night. I ran like I was running for my life. Escaping from Carol felt the same. I was experiencing a post-traumatic stress episode where I was feeling the same sense of oppression and imminent danger. The same overwhelming primal need to escape for my survival.

Out of breath, I rushed by a clock on the wall informing me I'd been evacuating Dr. Brenner's home for close to an hour. I was almost finished making sure I'd retrieved all my things when I heard her home phone ring again. I raced to the kitchen to hear if the caller would leave a message. It was Carol. She sounded unglued and frantic.

"Emma, answer this *fucking phone right now!* I've called

your office and *I know you've called in sick.* Pick up the phone, God dammit! I'm in-between patients right now. Don't you realize how important I am? I have patients who need me and I should be focusing on them. But instead, I'm having to check up on you to find out what *the hell* you're doing! Have you done those things I told you to do yet?! You had *better call me!*"

Her voice sickened me. She sounded like she'd transformed into a monster who held none of the charismatic, super-therapist qualities from previous times. I checked my messages from my work phone and listened to three more messages from her—all sounding the same. It was time to go. In fact, well past time to go.

Panting and sweating as I slipped behind the wheel of my loaded SUV, it occurred to me I'd left my wet clothes in her washing machine. I sucked in a breath and turned the car off. Jumping out, I ran to the downstairs level of Carol's house where her laundry room was located. My thoughts were to turn the dryer on and allow the clothes to get at least fifteen minutes of drying time. I was thinking to myself, "I have time, right?" I set the dryer for fifteen minutes and used the extra time to make a final sweep through Carol's three-level house making sure to not leave anything. I knew for sure I would never be coming back.

I did my final check in the kitchen. My gaze swept around the countertops, barstools, and then spotted Carol's home phone on the counter. The message light was blinking red. That's funny, I thought. I'd erased the earlier call from Carol. This was obviously a new one. I was thinking I must have been downstairs in the laundry room when she had possibly left another message. The voice in my head screamed *"Don't listen to it. Just get out of here!"* I hit the button anyway. Carol's recorded voice boomed through the kitchen making my gut clench even tighter. I stood in fear with the palm of my hand clamped tightly over my mouth.

"I'll have you know I've had to cancel my next client thanks to you not answering the phone! Have you done the things I told you to do?! I'm coming home and *we are going to talk!* I'll be there in five minutes." Carol was on her way.

Oh, shit! Looking out the large picture window from the kitchen, I could see the steep, winding street below. But the road was empty. And then I saw it. Carol's black Infiniti snaking its way up the slow ascent of the hill. I ran out of the kitchen with such speed I sprawled over Carol's dogs in the middle of the floor. After I righted myself, I practically jumped down the narrow staircase to get to the dryer where I could retrieve my still-damp clothes. I shoved them into my too-small laundry bag, which seemed to take forever. Wasting precious time. Time I did not have. My last moments at Carol Brenner's house were spent climbing the stairs two at a time before opening the garage door to bolt to my car, fling open the driver's door, and shamelessly screech out of the driveway.

As I haphazardly backed out, I took a stolen moment to look into my rearview mirror. Just as I slammed my Bronco out of reverse and into drive, I saw Carol's black Infinity closing the distance right behind me. Speeding up the road in the opposite direction from Carol's house seemed the smartest and safest thing to do. Meeting her face-to-face was a terror I didn't want to encounter. I was unsure of how erratic or hostile her behavior might burst into—and I didn't want to find out. I kept looking in my rearview mirror. She was not following me. I made it out just before her arrival back to the house. My panic was beginning to subside, but only slightly. I felt I'd just narrowly escaped from a prison camp and was breathing the first breaths of freedom I'd had in months. And, I'd just scarcely thwarted her plan to keep me in her all-consuming fire. When I got far enough away, I parked in a cul-de-sac in another neighborhood. Taking in deep breaths helped calm me. Then, placing my hand on my chest comforted me. I smiled a slow smile of relief and satisfaction realizing I'd done absolutely none of the demands on Carol's to-do list.

17
EDUCATION

Rick had given me a key to the new rental house just up the hill from our old one. He had said to come back as soon as I was ready and we'd work things out. I was unsure about that, but knew I had to sever the exploitative, cultic, one-on-one abusive relationship Dr. Brenner had entrapped me in. I knew Rick was not a great choice, but he was the lesser of the two evils. It was a depressing winding drive up the canyon road lined with burned and charred ground with homes that hadn't been touched since the fire over a month ago. Dr. Brenner had placed me in her fire and fully intended to leave me there until all that was left of me were charred remains. Maybe the same thing had happened to Maria.

After putting all my things away, I sat in the middle of my new rental house living room floor crying. Unraveling. What had I done? I felt blame and shame creeping over me. Shame at allowing myself to be possessed by my psychologist. Shame at what I'd done to Rick. Shame at how unreliable and undependable I'd become at my job. I felt like a stranger to myself.

My cats swished their furry bodies and tails around me

and on top of me letting me know how I'd been missed. I buried my tear-stained face into each one as they continued to welcome me home. Home. Was I home? I was unsure of everything and anything. I had the overwhelming awareness that I needed help. This was going to be too substantial for me to handle on my own. When Rick later mentioned we needed to find a counselor who could help me deprogram from the damage my psychologist had caused, I knew he was right.

"And there's something else, Emma. I found an attorney. We need to talk about reporting her to the board of ethics *and* file a civil lawsuit." Rick paused for my response.

"What? No, wait! I can't do that. It was my fault, too. She didn't hold a gun to my head. I promised her I'd never report her!" I confessed.

"Wait—Carol actually told you to *never report her?!*" Rick's eyebrows shot up in shock and surprise. He leaned his body toward mine and continued. "Emma, she took an oath, the Hippocratic oath 'to do no harm.' She uses her position of power to abuse, and then get her victims to believe the unethicalness was all their fault. Don't you see this same thing happened to her other client, *Maria?* And did you know that *Gail was also Brenner's former patient* before they purchased their home together?"

"So why did no one else report her?" I didn't know Gail had also been a former patient.

"Because she's a master manipulator, Emma. She's no different than a sociopathic cult leader who uses a fear based, punishment and reward system to keep their victims under their control. There's also the fact that reporting her and filing a suit is an enormous undertaking. The whole process could take years. It will bring the whole experience back up for you and her attorney will try to discredit us both. But especially you." Rick admitted.

I countered with, "But who am I to make her lose her license? How could I do that to her? I promised her I wouldn't be like Maria."

"Emma, if Maria or Gail, and whoever else she's exploited and violated ... *Dammit*, that sociopath has been using her entire client population as her pool for selection and grooming! If any of them had done the right thing by coming forth —maybe this would never have happened to you."

I began reflecting on how she'd insist our relationship was different because we loved each other and the rules didn't apply. I started to see how this was yet another way of her justifying her repeated unethical behavior, by saying the rules apply to others, but not to her. In later research on the tactics of exploitative therapists, I read the work of cult expert Dr. Janja Lalich, who wrote "You would have had to become a steel robot to not have succumbed to those pressures." Dr. Lalich also wrote that "It's our deepest Self that gets turned inside out" by a cultic abusive relationship. This resonated.

Rick handed me more information he'd found online about the exploitation of clients by their therapists. I began to read: "Unfortunately, recovery can easily be compounded by the fact that many therapists, social workers, and other mental health professionals have no experience in deprogramming a victim coming out of a cultic relationship. Depression and relationship problems are among the biggest problems. Moshe Spiro, a therapist, observes: 'intensive psychotherapy is suitable, if not mandatory, for successful de-regression from cultic commitment, for return of adaptive cognitive and emotional functioning, and to expose the exploitee to more healthy reintegration into normal living.'"

My escape from Dr. Brenner's house had been fueled by my intense anger and fear. However, my flight response had started to wear off by the following day. The feelings of intense attachment were seeping back in, and my clarity waned. My rational mind was trying to hold on to the full truth of what she'd done. But it was my deepest trauma, my primal wound, that desperately needed to hold on to the fantasy of Carol Brenner as the nurturing mother I never had. For me, *that* was the location of the wound in which the infection had settled in. Paradoxically, I was led to see her as a beautiful nurturing light who shone brightly. That her light —the one only she could provide—would protect and heal me. She deceitfully convinced me I needed to stand in the light with her—which were actually flames—to consume me. I was not healed enough yet, after just fleeing her, to be able to see the distortions of my own thinking. I was actually missing and grieving the loss of her! The loss of her, the loss of who I wanted her to be, and who she'd pretended to be. But I knew I needed another counselor who could help me undo the deep damage.

Our new attorney, who specialized in medical and doctor malpractice cases, had given us some recommendations for a new counselor. By the time I went to see her, a few weeks after I left Dr. Brenner, I was depressed to the point of being almost mute. I didn't have the energy or desire to breathe in enough air to support talking above a whisper, or a mumble. The aftermath of leaving Dr. Brenner was almost worse than when she had her grip on me. My progress of deprogramming from the mental and emotional influence Dr. Brenner had over me was painful and slow. I was not able to cope with everyday life and because I was still extremely distorted by who Dr. Brenner truly was, I took an extended disability leave from work. I had difficulty concentrating and day-to-day tasks seemed impossible.

A few months after seeing the new counselor, whose job it was to help me begin breaking the mind reform Dr. Brenner had subjected me to, she encouraged me to consider taking an antidepressant. I refused – I'd tried more than a few antidepressants in the past and had experienced intense anxiety and even suicidal ideation. I decided instead to explore taking master's level psychology courses in hopes of educating myself about what had happened to me. Going to class, reading the material, and having to be more social started to slowly bring me out of the heavy depression I'd been in since my escape from Carol Brenner.

I was horrified one day when I picked up my home phone and heard her familiar hypnotic voice.

"Emma, how are you? I've missed you. I'm *devastated* without you. Let's talk about this—it's really been a huge misunderstanding. You don't want me to lose my license, do you?! We've meant so much to each other."

And then, in her best super-therapist voice, she said, "Don't you see how the act of you leaving me is just your *unconscious re-enacting your birth mother leaving you?*"

Even after all the education I'd immersed myself in to rid my mind of her psychological power and influence, I still buckled at the sound of her voice. Simultaneous sensations of fear, nausea, and yes, deep yearning washed over me. I felt myself starting to get small again, my heart racing, and my breath growing shallow. I quickly hung up the phone.

Our attorney had warned me that once she received the letters from her certification boards, she would probably try to make contact. I was not to answer any questions and to refuse to engage in any conversation. The letters from the Board of Psychology and the Board of Social Workers would fully inform her of the allegations filed against her. Specifically, the allegations *I* was making against *her*. I was supported by Rick, our attorney, and my new therapist, who all helped me to see I was doing the right thing. Sometimes I absolutely believed this; other times I felt I was betraying her. I kept hearing her voice: "You wanted this relationship every bit as much as I did—you were operating from your own free will." While I was under her influence, I believed this to be true. I even told her my feelings for her were not due to any transference I was having with her. But how could I have been operating with agency over my life when my psychologist had taken and twisted my innermost thoughts and vulnerabilities and set them on fire, and then watched me sit in the flames?

UNMASKING THE SOCIOPATH

After completing the first semester of my master's program in psychology, Rick and I were feeling strong enough to finally make the doctor's appointment with an infertility specialist. Within a few months we were ecstatic to learn we were pregnant. I loved being pregnant and felt connected to the life growing inside me from the very beginning. Things were slowly starting to look and feel better. At my insistence, Rick had also promised to get a tax attorney and to finally clean up his unpaid tax bills. My depression began lifting. I enjoyed my psychology studies and the ideas and concepts I was learning were starting to make my own life make sense. When my parents learned I was pregnant, we reconciled after many years of estrangement, and they flew in for a visit. Things were still difficult between us, but we had restored the relationship enough to admit we cared about each other.

Living so close to Carol Brenner was a constant reminder of the horrible physical and psychological abuse she'd put us through. Living among homes which were burned to the ground and had little to no vegetation left due to the fire was depressing. There was a steady flow of noisy construction trucks coming in and out of the neighborhood, adding to my already nauseous state. We began to worry our surroundings were not conducive to a healthy pregnancy. At five months pregnant, Rick and I broke our lease agreement and moved to a city a few miles inland.

We continued the slow-moving process of unmasking Dr. Brenner, finding the Board of Psychology and the Board of Behavioral Science (Social Work) members seemed to put the burden of proof on me. This was both difficult and disheartening, and often retraumatized me and impeded my recovery. I was still having difficulty maintaining my clarity and would slip back into thinking I needed Carol Brenner for my survival. There was not adequate therapy for me when I left my cultic one-on-one abusive relationship with her. I did the best I could with the therapist I had but it became clear that my counselor was not equipped or experienced in the type of counseling I needed to deprogram me. And what about all the presenting issues I went into therapy for in the first place? Those had been compounded by Dr. Brenner's unethical therapy, and I subsequently walked away with new problems, plus the old ones.

Educating myself on the tactics used by charismatic, authoritarian, totalitarian leaders with certain mental disorders to attract their victims was key to my recovery. I learned that they first prey on individuals who are in a transitional period of their lives where they can be more easily manipulated to have a blind obedience to authority. I had (and always will have) the complicated and complex early childhood trauma known as the primal wound. The early separation from my birth mom caused attachment issues and neurological adaptations to occur in me to survive. Subsequently, being placed in a home where I developed a notably high Adverse Childhood Experiences (ACE) score, further complicated my way of being in the world. When a predator like Dr. Brenner saw me in the driveway that day, she already knew she was going to seduce me. While anyone could have been manipulated and deceived by her persuasive coercion, my background and emotional state were particularly ideal for what she had in mind.

The waters in which I swam in my youth conditioned me to think of myself as lesser than. I was deceived to believe that loyalty and humility exist only at the expense of Self. Even if it caused me to betray my deepest sense of self. The correlation of being relinquished at birth and adopted by parents who operated with an authoritarian power dynamic, and then being indoctrinated, deceived, and manipulated by a cultic therapist became obvious to me. However, I had no established "pre-cult" sense of self to return to. The trademarks of a cultic relationship include coercive persuasion, mind reform, gaslighting, abuse of positions of power, and the use of a punishment and reward system to foster an attachment and unhealthy dependency upon the egocentric abuser. American psychiatrist and author Robert J. Lifton says "with greater knowledge about cultic relationships, people are less susceptible to deception." Margaret Singer, author of *Cults in Our Midst*, along with Janja Lalich, Ph.D., in a 1996 study of cults writes "The cult-like experience is often a conflicted one with profound confusion." These definitions could have been written just for me.

The healthier I became, the more shame I felt. How could I have let this happen to me? How could I have been so blind to her pervasive persuasion? But I had to admit it was only easier to see in light of all the research I'd done. Awareness was key. My self-talk kept telling me how stupid I had been, how gullible. Years later, I would discover an interesting phenomenon called Genetic Sexual Attraction in Adoption Reunion Relationships: it is a physiological and psychological response to meeting a relative that an individual was not raised with. Some speculate that this genetic attraction syndrome can result from attachment issues and trying to connect. A person who lost a parent (primarily a mother) at, or close to birth, didn't complete the entire birthing process. Many of the necessary hormonal processes didn't take place due to removing the infant from the mother before those physiological and neurological developments took place. "Variations in qualities of mother–infant relationships among humans thus appear to have deep biological roots in the form of their capacity to shape children's psychological and biological responses to their environment—effects that extend into adulthood," writes Myron Hofer, who was director of the Sackler Institute for Developmental Psychology at Columbia University until his retirement in 2011.

When I lost my first year of the symbiotic mother/child relationship, that meant I did not have skin-to-skin contact, or the essential hormone oxytocin, which helps bond mother and child. I believe I was unconsciously trying to connect with Dr. Brenner and have her fill the needs I had never gotten as a newborn and beyond. I was stripped of this critical physiological and neurological process that is vital for healthy development.

This was the Achilles' heel Dr. Carol Brenner spotted in me. She then abused her position of power and used tactics not unlike those of predators who groom and traffic their prey.

~

"Emma, our attorney called. You're not going to like what he had to say." Rick's lined and weathered face looked serious.

"Oh, no! What now?" I was frustrated by all we'd gone through with attorneys, hearings, testimony, and the slow action taken by the licensing boards.

"Brenner's attorney has a subpoena for your journals. The court is saying you must produce them so they can enter them into evidence by tomorrow."

"What? Those are private! What about patient/therapist confidentiality?" I cried.

"Apparently, when you sue your therapist, confidentiality is off the table." Rick looked just as angry about this development as I was. I kept thinking of how twisted it was that Carol would want my innermost thoughts and feelings to be entered into the case so all could see. But then again, didn't that highlight how little she was thinking of me, her patient, instead of herself?

I plunked down into the soft armchair, letting all the air escape from my lungs. Rubbing my round belly, I remarked, "But my journals wouldn't prove anything other than how she manipulated me. What I wrote tells the story of how she slowly and methodically fostered a dependency and attachment to her."

"Emma, it will be her malpractice attorney's job to discredit you in any way possible. He'll probably take things out of context and then try to turn them around to look like it's your fault." Rick took a swig of his coffee. We'd both quit smoking before the pregnancy. Coffee—*more coffee*, was now his vice.

"I'll burn it. I'll say I don't have my journal anymore." I said stubbornly. But even as I said the words, I knew I was going to have to hand it over to the court. My mind was reeling, trying to remember the exact things I'd confessed in my journal, writings I had thought no one else would ever have the right to see.

"We don't want to risk obstructing justice and being held

in contempt of the court. It could sabotage all your efforts of trying to expose her as an unethical therapist who exploits her patients."

I leaned forward in the chair trying to get the momentum to get to my feet. My pregnant belly was in the way. Once on my feet, I said, "Fine. I'll go get it."

19

DEVIL'S ATTORNEY

January 1997, mediation

"So, Mrs. Stevens ... You are married to Rick Stevens, who's here in the room with us today?" Dr. Brenner's attorney looked at me with one eyebrow raised.

"Yes. That's correct," I responded.

"Good. Good. May I call you by your first name? Would that be alright?" He questioned again with head down, looking at his notes.

"Yes. That would be fine," I answered.

"Do you understand, Emma, that you're under oath and will be held in contempt if you're found to be not telling the truth?" Dr. Brenner's malpractice attorney finally made eye contact with me when he said the words "contempt" and "tell the truth." I realized he was trying to intimidate and unnerve me. He was doing a great job.

I had bought a new suit for the mediation hearing, a slate gray blazer with black buttons, and a matching skirt. My objective was to look professional. And I would have—if the skirt hadn't been accidentally altered an inch and half too short. I had only discovered the too-short length that morning when getting dressed for the hearing. Left with no other option, I wore the suit.

My chair was positioned in front of the room facing the defense table, where Dr. Brenner and her attorney were sitting. I had no table or anything else obstructing my frontal view. In a seated position, the length of my skirt caused me much unease and feelings of self-consciousness. It was difficult enough to see her for the first time in almost three years, but my plan to look professional probably missed the mark. While I diligently tried not looking at her, my body was having a visceral reaction to her energy in the room. I loathed myself at that moment. The thought that I may still have some of her tentacles attached to me.

I answered the defense attorney in the affirmative that I realized I was under oath. So far, his questions had been straightforward. But I had a foreboding that his line of questioning was about to follow the Perry Mason paradigm of 'ambush by deposition.' My brain and central nervous system were in such a fight or flight state that wouldn't take much for a skilled attorney to catch me by surprise and tie me up in my own words.

"Emma, is it true that your husband, Rick Stevens, has a sizable unpaid tax bill owed to the Internal Revenue Service? And with a poor credit score, you and Mr. Stevens have been restricted to renting homes since your relationship began around eight years ago?"

Oh, no, I thought. Why would they be bringing this up? I'd confided this information to Dr. Brenner during the course of my therapy sessions. It was one of my most agonizing concerns about Rick. His procrastination traits and his inability to take responsibility.

"Yes," I answered.

"And isn't it true, Emma, that you and your husband

knew that Dr. Carol Brenner is of significant financial means and that you targeted her, making these allegations to extort money from her and ruin her good name?"

No one had prepared me for outlandish accusations such as this. I was shocked. Stunned. I answered with a sharp shake of my head and a huff, *"No!"*

"Mrs. Stevens ... Oh, I'm sorry, *Emma.* Do you recognize this item?" The attorney asked.

I lost my breath.

"Emma, do you understand the question I've asked? Do you recognize it?" He kept the item lifted high in the air for effect while staring at me accusingly, awaiting my answer.

I self-consciously tried smoothing down my skirt as if to lengthen it by the inch and half it was missing.

"Yes. It's my journal." Fear and embarrassment flooded me. I momentarily forgot about my worry of a too-short skirt and started focusing on the uncomfortable feeling of the heat and blood pulsating in my face. My vision became distorted, my heartbeat pounded in my ears, and that familiar feeling of being off-balance when I was under Dr. Brenner's influence returned.

"OK. Good. So, this is your journal. Can you please read to everyone this highlighted portion I've placed on the over-head?" His full attention was on me. Panic was rising through my body like a torch setting me on fire.

I read from the overhead, "Journal entry, August 9, 1993: I bumped into my next-door neighbor again today. She's a psychologist. I asked her about counseling and whether she'd consider seeing me, or if she knew of anyone she could refer me to. I was happy when she gave me her card to make an appointment."

"Thank you, Emma." Dr. Brenner's attorney seemed to be studying something on the desk in front of him. I used this time to think hard about how he was going to twist my journal statements to be in Dr. Brenner's favor. It was difficult staying present when my body was feeling the shame of having my private journal be read. His questions were taken out of context. And he was leading me to answer them in just the way he wanted me to.

"Is it true you asked that question of Dr. Brenner because you knew you'd be asking her to break her boundaries by accepting you as a patient?"

"No, that's *not* true. I didn't know anything about counseling at that time. I was only asking if it would be a problem or not." I was letting her attorney rattle me.

"So, Emma, is it your testimony that you've never been in counseling before?" Dr. Brenner's attorney looked ready to pounce on me.

"No, I didn't say *that* either. You're twisting my words!"

"Emma, please just answer the questions." The defense attorney shot me a warning glare. "Have you ever been to counseling prior to seeking the services of Dr. Brenner?"

"I went for a few sessions my senior year in college," I said.

"I see, and what did you go to see a counselor for during college?"

My anger was rising. I had no idea what this line of questioning was to prove.

"I was engaged to be married but felt I wasn't ready to take that step. Talking with my therapist helped me gain the strength to admit I didn't want to get married. And so, I didn't. I broke up with him."

The defense attorney suddenly looked straight up at me, then down again at his notes, and then settled on staring blankly at me again.

"Just a few more things, Emma. Would you now read this next excerpt from your journal dated November 19, 1993, please?"

I quickly pre-read the paragraph wondering how out of context it was going to be.

Taking a deep breath in, I read, "I've really grown to love and trust her. I now wonder what I'd ever do without her. I'd do anything to be with her."

"Emma, can you please clarify to the court who you're saying you love, can't be without, and would do *anything* to be with?"

I hated that he was going to make me say her name. I had to pause and breathe before uttering her name.

"Dr. Brenner."

"Emma, can you please state for the testimony the full name of the person you're speaking of? And please speak clearly so we can all hear you."

I couldn't believe he was going to make me say her name —again. I felt such hate in that moment not only for Dr. Brenner, but also for her attorney.

"Dr. Carol Brenner." The room was silent.

Dr. Brenner's attorney didn't look up from his notes. There was a long, awkward pause. Then he followed with, "Isn't it true, Emma, that you planned that first meeting in your driveway with Dr. Brenner? And that you already knew she was a well-respected psychologist?"

"What? No! How would I know she was a psychologist? It was completely by accident that I got home from work that day at the same time she did. I was just on my driveway, which was right next to hers, getting my mail from the mail-box." Panic and fear caused my shoulders to tense and the pitch of my voice to rise.

"Isn't it true, Emma, that you had planned this relation-ship from the beginning and your motivation was to *conquer the therapist?*" Dr. Brenner's attorney let his words just hang in the air—dressing them up as truth.

For me, all the air in my lungs had dispelled and left me

with a deflated, crumpled, and trampled feeling. This just was not true. I was unsure of how to express myself so everyone in the room, especially the mediator, would believe me.

I responded with a simple, exasperated "No."

Then, I suddenly remembered. I remembered something very joyous I'd just confirmed earlier that same morning. I was pregnant again. Rick and I loved our little girl so much, who was then close to a year and a half old, and we wanted to try for at least one more child. Remembering my newly confirmed pregnant condition helped me get myself more regulated and less upset by whatever the defense attorney was throwing at me. Being a new mother to my little girl, and now the hope of having another child, was *my* super-power. No matter what this attorney said or didn't say was not going to take that joy away from me.

Dr. Brenner's malpractice attorney came at me with many things that day but ended with the fact that I'd given Dr. Brenner a key to our home so she could feed our cats while Rick and I were away one weekend.

"Emma, isn't it true you *willingly* gave Dr. Brenner a key to your home?

I took a deep breath before answering. "Yes, but …"

Her attorney cut me off. "Please just answer the question with either yes, or no."

Feeling boxed in by his question, I said, "Yes."

He continued, "And, isn't it true that you had invited her to come over any time?"

"Yes," I answered. Frustrated, but I had to answer that this was a true statement again.

And then he concluded with, "And isn't it *also* true that on —or about December 3, 1993—you asked Dr. Brenner to move all your things from your home over to hers?"

"No, I did not!" I stated emphatically. He was trying to

suggest she hadn't entered my home uninvited and proceeded to take all my personal belongings to move into her own home next-door. But he was no longer listening. All he wanted to establish was, at one time, I had *willingly* given Dr. Carol Brenner a key to my home.

20

RETRAUMATIZED

At about the same time as the civil lawsuit hearing in 1997, almost four years after I escaped from Dr. Brenner, the state Board of Psychology ruled to revoke Dr. Brenner's license to practice as a psychologist in the state of California. While I was relieved at this news, I was equally dismayed and frustrated by the Board of Social Workers who only put her on probation with minimal requirements and length of time to become fully reinstated.

"I've got some news," our attorney said. "We've found Maria, another patient Dr. Brenner exploited. But after speaking with her mother, I don't think we can expect her to be willing to testify. She's not psychologically well enough, her mother informed me." Our attorney was trying to get and find another witness to come forth. If we could, our civil case would be much stronger.

"But what about the fact that the whole reason Maria can't testify is because of the mental and sexual abuse Dr. Brenner put her through instead of trying to help her?!" I said with my arm muscles tightened and fists clenched.

"It won't help our case without a formal statement from

116

Maria, or Gail, her most recent unethical, dual relationship. And they are both unwilling, *or* unable, to do either," our attorney replied apologetically.

I couldn't help feeling angry with both Maria and Gail. If they had come forth, there was a good chance Dr. Brenner would not have been able to abuse me.

The truth is, Dr. Carol Brenner is unhealthy, if not very sick herself, with the sociopathic trademarks of egocentricity, narcissistic traits, extreme selfishness, coercive persuasion, charisma, and grandiosity. All are consistent with personality disorders. No one assessed the situation to protect not only her patients, but to protect her from herself.

The last-ditch effort of Dr. Brenner's malpractice attorney during the civil trial was to present the idea that Dr. Brenner had not crossed any therapeutic boundaries with me in our therapy sessions prior to October 27, 1993, the day of the Laguna Beach fire. The defense proposed that the defendant, Dr. Brenner, had suffered Post Traumatic Stress Disorder (PTSD), due to the fire and her actions of misconduct were the direct result of this trauma.

"Emma, isn't it true Dr. Brenner talked to you many times about the appropriate boundaries of the therapeutic relationship between patient and therapist?"

"Yes, she did." I stated simply. This question made me want to smirk with the knowledge of just how many inappropriate unethical therapist/patient relationships she confessed to me of having. Including Paul, the Ford car salesman.

"And isn't it true it was only after the fire that the boundaries were crossed?"

I jumped at the opportunity to prove him wrong in his leading statement.

"No. That's *not* true." By the time of the trial, in 1997, I was well into my master's coursework in psychology. I had learned of the terms and definitions used to describe what the healthy boundaries of the therapeutic relationship entail. And Dr. Brenner had broken every one of them.

"The dual relationship and the inappropriate physical contact initiated by Dr. Brenner started well before the fire," I said adamantly.

"Explain please." Dr. Brenner's attorney had just presented me with the opportunity to speak of the intimate hugs she had incorporated into all my therapy sessions.

"The hugs given by Dr. Brenner were—at first—only at the end of every session. But over time, she began giving me hugs at the beginning *and* the end of every session. Then, the duration of the hugs began getting longer and longer. And more intimate." I was happy to have been given the opportunity to bring this into the mediation since I had always felt the excessive physical contact was one of the main ways she had indoctrinated me. Specifically, since I had been oxytocin deprived at birth due to relinquishment and not being properly nurtured throughout my childhood. This is how she led me into her fire.

"Did you ask her to stop?" Said Dr. Brenner's attorney accusingly.

My adrenaline surged. I wanted to scream at him. I wanted to leap from my chair and onto the table positioned in front of Dr. Brenner and her attorney and point my finger. *"You! You did this! I hate you!"*

Instead, I replied, "I was already under her influence by then. She knew what she was doing. Her hugs were insidious. Starting out benign. And then, before I knew it, I thought I'd die if she didn't put her arms around me."

Another long, awkward pause ensued. Up until that moment, I had made sure to avoid eye contact with Dr. Brenner. Oops. Too late. There she was staring at me with her super-therapist gaze and demeanor. She enjoyed hearing my words of what must have sounded like worship and praise to her. I watched as she held her head half-cocked, peering over her black-rimmed glasses, and looking at me in a haughty, condescending way. She then leaned over with a wry grin and whispered something into her attorney's ear.

Finally, her attorney looked up and said, "When did you first know you were a lesbian, Emma?"

That was it. My window of emotional tolerance had been exceeded, and it was reminiscent of the repeated, slow-motion, full-wind-up slaps that were delivered to me by my mother for the duration of my childhood. This triggered within me a crying jag that I'm certain looked to Dr. Brenner and her attorney as if I were agreeing that I was a lesbian. But the possibility of me being a lesbian was not what triggered my crying response. It was the method in which it was delivered. The attorney's approach, which I was convinced was orchestrated by Dr. Brenner, was a symbolic slap to knock me off my feet, and to flood me with self-doubt by questioning my sexuality. Who knew better how to do this than Dr. Brenner, who I'd confessed all my weaknesses and fears to? It was also a way to further damage my marriage. To destabilize Rick's and my relationship.

I was instructed by the mediator to not answer the question. I was relieved since I was unsure how anyone would understand me through my tears and constricted, choked voice. I stole one last glance at the defense table and saw they looked pleased even though I had been instructed to not answer their question. They had unnerved me—which was their objective.

21
THE OFFER

My attorney concluded the mediation. "This is the most egregious case of misconduct and malpractice by a therapist I've worked on in my 20-year practice." He went on to say how Dr. Brenner's breach of the Hippocratic Oath, an oath of ethics historically taken by physicians to "first, do no harm," had been severely and utterly ignored. The boundaries had been crossed one calculated choice at a time. He laid the blame squarely on Dr. Brenner for accepting me or Rick as patients, given we were her next-door neighbors. This dual relationship, being both our next-door neighbor and our therapist, was against the ethical guidelines especially when she didn't uphold the healthy boundaries of the therapeutic relationship. Our attorney highlighted that it was at that point, when I had initially asked for help finding a counselor, Dr. Brenner should have referred me to another therapist.

"The insidious and unethical way Dr. Brenner invaded my client Emma Stevens' life and marriage was comparable to the way a sexual predator lures a child into an abusive, sexual relationship. She used her imbalance of power and charismatic methods to indoctrinate Emma into a type of cultic, one-on-one relationship. Dr. Brenner repeatedly told Emma to not tell anyone of their secret relationship that had developed both inside and outside the therapeutic boundaries because she *knew* what others would think of her intentional gross negligence. She also knew how to warp Emma's mind through first demanding her vulnerability, and then fostering an emotional dependency upon Dr. Brenner. She encouraged the dual relationship well before the Laguna fire on October 27, 1993, by having Emma come over to her home and engage in social activities on several occasions. Not to mention the unethicalness of having Emma join her in the counseling room for a private phone therapy session which was for another patient."

Our attorney paused for a drink of water and continued. "Emma came to see Dr. Brenner with the presenting symptoms of marital problems, infertility, childhood trauma, relinquishment, and adoption-related issues. None of these were addressed by Dr. Brenner. In fact, Dr. Brenner blatantly ignored my client's issues and decided to instead, exploit them to her own advantage. She actively set out to destroy Emma and Rick's marriage to expressively pave the way to enable Dr. Brenner to move Emma into her own home, making Emma her partner."

In my mind, body, and soul, I interpreted our attorney's words inside my head as, "making Emma her prisoner."

In the proverbial last hour before taking the case in front of a jury, the defense attorney offered to settle out of court. Our attorney whisked us into a private room to discuss our options.

"The defense team is ready to make you an offer to avoid

a jury trial. I think it's a good deal. It could be risky going in front of a jury because they can oftentimes be very fickle. And most people aren't educated about the detrimental psychological effects an exploitive therapist can have on an individual. As you've probably been able to tell, the mediator we've been assigned is *also* uneducated of the psychological effects of a predator who holds an unequal balance of power over an individual. It's because of this prevailing ignorance that you could walk away with nothing." His words hit me with a visceral feeling in my gut.

"But what about how I've lost my job because of her?! And now I have to go to another therapist to undo what she, the therapist, did to me?" These things were all true, and I knew my attorney knew it, too. I was facing a long road to recovery. It would turn out to be decades of recovery.

I accepted the offer from Dr. Brenner's defense attorney, but with a heavy heart, feeling I had somehow given up or outright lost. While the settlement offer was close to $100,000, it could never be enough to alleviate or wipe away the pain and damage she caused.

"Emma, you've done *what you can* do. You've been embroiled in a civil court case since 1994, you've filed your complaints with all the certification boards she's certified with, and you've stood strong. You should walk away from this now and focus on your growing family. Congratulations, by the way! When's the baby due?" My attorney remarked.

"October!" Being reminded of my pregnancy always made me happy. "I guess it's hard to let go and think there's not something else I could be doing to make sure she doesn't exploit someone else."

"And that's out of your control," Rick punctuated.

I started trying to find a sense of peace and freedom in that thought. It was time to begin a newer, deeper degree of letting go. One unfortunate byproduct of taking Dr. Brenner to court and trying to hold her accountable was that I could not completely let it go. Not yet. I had to think about, discuss, and even see Dr. Brenner during the multiple days of mediation. I had to be cross-examined by her malpractice attorney and retraumatized by his statements that were meant to discredit, disrupt, and disturb me. I was forced to justify the things I'd written in my journal that I had thought were confidential. The waiting for court dates, the post-poned court dates, documents to be signed, evidence to be gathered, all of these and more prevented Rick, me, and our daughter, Dana, from moving forward. And now that the time had finally arrived, it proved to be even harder than I had thought.

22

TIME IS BENDY

January 2023, almost 30 years later

From the end of the civil suit mediation and the petitioning of the ethics boards until now, time has been assuredly bendy. My healing has been far from linear, as healing seldom is, and my therapy was put on hold for many years after the birth of my children. However, when I finally woke up to my life—I walked into it singing! It's ironic, but maybe not so unique, that my healing came from crashing into my rock bottom. In the years following the court proceedings, my alcohol use had steadily increased. After drinking alcohol excessively landed me in the hospital twice to detox, followed by a stellar counselor who had the guts to tell me I was an alcoholic, my beautiful paths of reclaiming my life began in earnest. It has been more than six years now.

It wasn't easy to trust another therapist, to do the necessary, but seemingly impossible, task of becoming vulnerable. I still question my physical and emotional safety behind the closed door of a therapy session. I have visceral reactions to the intimacy of being separated from the outside world. And then there's the feelings of, "Am I overly attached to my therapist?" "Do I feel I'd ever be coerced to allow him or her to move me into their home and make me their mate?" Now working with two therapists who are undoubtedly ethically and morally above reproach, and with whom I have the healthiest of rapport, I still question my motives—and sometimes theirs, too. It's residual trauma that I'm still working through.

What does a stellar therapist look like? I've learned the hard way what the danger signs of a therapist who's out to get their own needs met are. And the tricky thing is that it's not always obvious. And it's even less obvious for someone like me who hadn't been allowed any sort of boundaries in my youth. The authoritative parental structure I was to conform to did not allow personal boundaries to exist. If they had, then the result could have been anarchy. For that to have happened, my parents would have had to be different people. Here's what I now expect from my therapists or counselors:

- Boundaries/mentally, physically, and spiritually
- Rapport
- Empathy/Sympathy
- That they also have a therapist/ *"physician, heal thyself"*
- Encourages patient to have agency
- Continuing education/Up-to-date researched modalities of therapy
- Patient centered/Not therapist centered
- Attentive

- Patient is always encouraged to speak without fear of judgment or abandonment
- The therapist is of good standing with the licensing board(s) of certification

And even still, my healing has been a process, especially as an adopted person. Having been adopted, my truth often comes in layers. One layer was to give myself permission to tell my story, but under a pseudonym. And another confusing layer, that may sound curious, is that I pay tribute to my *fictitious* self, Emma, as the true writer of my story. I have difficulty believing that *I, myself,* wrote and published my story. This puzzling notion smacks of residual self-esteem issues. Sigh, more work to be done! There are other meaningful reasons I've chosen to write with anonymity—mainly to protect my family who is far from ready, or will ever be ready, to hear my truth. My hope is to merge my author persona someday soon with all my parts of self who make up who I am. To fully step into my truth.

One of the main takeaways I have pieced together from growing up in a cult-like family and a society that treats adoptees as commodities, is that I now realize I had no "pre-cult" self. Dr. Janja Lalich, a respected and awarded expert of cultic experiences, author of *Take Back Your Life: Recovering from Cults and Abusive Relationships,* describes "The main features of a 'totalistic' control cult, which can also be just one person: 'They espouse an all-encompassing belief system,' 'exhibit excessive devotion to the leader,' 'avoid criticism of the leader,' and 'feel disdain' for anyone who doesn't fit their plan." When first reading this, I had to admit it sounded familiar from everything from my oppressive childhood, to the way society views and treats adoptees, to my marriage to Rick—who was narcissistic, manipulative, and deceiving—to my indoctrination by Dr. Brenner. It's like I had unknowingly been a *cult hopper*, going from one oppressive, totalitarian relationship to the next.

23

AUTHENTICITY VS. ATTACHMENT

M any years have passed since the awful days of my childhood trauma, the Laguna Beach fire, and the mental and emotional entanglement I had with Dr. Brenner. The inner haunting from Dr. Brenner taking possession of my mind was not resolved in days, months, or even years after my well-executed escape. Almost 30 years later, Dr. Carol Brenner is still in private practice operating under her Social Worker license for $300 an hour.

Rick and I remained married until our children were eight and ten years old. He had blatantly dodged yet another tax bill that landed him in trouble with the IRS—again. He had lied to me about it and the other problems in our marriage had become insurmountable. Fortunately, my tax attorney helped me complete an Internal Revenue form called "Innocent Spouse Relief" that exempted me from Rick's wrongdoings. Rick also personally spent the entire monetary award from my civil lawsuit to pay a dental surgeon to try and correct the years of neglect he had done to his teeth. He ultimately had to have most of his teeth pulled and then used the rest of the money for dental implants. When that money ran out, he seemed to feel no remorse and allowed the delinquent bill to go to collections. There was never any college funding or any other support set aside for his children. Rick said he expected my parents to cover those needs.

I not only became a divorced single parent of two young children but began my recovery journey for multiple adverse experiences. A repressed sexual violence victimization in college, alcoholism, complex post-traumatic stress, and relinquishment and adoption trauma. Added to this list was recovering from the psychological and sexual abuse from Dr. Brenner. I've learned from my 12 step Alcoholics Anonymous (AA) program, Adult Children of Alcoholics & Dysfunctional Families (ACOA), Cognitive Therapy, Eye Movement Desensitization & Reprocessing (EMDR) therapy, Adoption Support Groups, and much self-reflection, that my journeys will be lifelong. I wholeheartedly accept this because it's the only path of continued discovery and exploration.

I cherish my sobriety and am thankful every day for the spiritual awakening it has brought. One AA slogan (and there are many!) says, "Are you sick and tired of being sick and tired?" And my answer was a resounding *yes*. It was only through sobriety—from alcohol and learning of emotional sobriety, which is similar to emotional maturity, or emotional intelligence, that I was able to start the necessary stripping away of the multidimensional layers to get to the core of all my issues. And it became clear that it was relinquishment, adoption, and having been shaped and formed by emotionally immature parents. I was not well taken care of in my youth. My trauma was ignored by my family which resulted in disenfranchised grief. This is to say that, as a closed-file adoptee, my first parents, and lineage, all died on the day I was born. This was a pain buried deep in my body and I was not allowed to grieve or even acknowledge. This resulted in a pervasive, unconscious feeling of deprivation. My work has been immersed in deprogramming and deconditioning from all the conscious and unconscious adaptations I had to do for survival.

Gabor Maté, a Hungarian Canadian physician and author, believes in the connection between mind and body health. He has stated, "When a child is born, a child has two needs. The first need is for attachment. Attachment is a huge need. The parents must attach with the infant and the infant must attach to the parents. We have to connect; we have to belong. It's just a basic human need. If we don't, the infant doesn't survive. But we have another need, as well, which is for authenticity. Authenticity is also a huge survival need for the capacity to know who we are, know what we feel, express who we are, and manifest who we are in our relationships and activities. This was an evolutionary need for survival in the wild. But what happens to a child where the attachment need is not compatible with the need for authenticity? In other words, if I'm authentic—my parents will reject me."

I suppressed my authenticity to survive childhood and then continued suppressing emotions well into adulthood. It's no wonder I didn't have a clue of who I was. It was the ignoring of my truth that caused the deep rift and pain of separation from Self. Not knowing myself set me up for the need to be on multiple journeys of recovery. These are recovery journeys for which I'm forever grateful. They are life giving and have presented me with choices I never knew I had. All of them give me permission to express my authenticity and take up space unapologetically. The only requirement is that I maintain a willingness to remain willing to evolve and change.

I'm reminded that having and trying to live this kind of

mantra is like attempting to swim upstream in unpopulated waters. When and *if* you get there, there won't be many others for you to swim with. It's not a way of being in the world that follows the path of least resistance. Following a more prophetic path seems to require an acceptance of reality's nature being of "unstable stability." It is the only *real* stability, because it's a truthful map of the tragic nature of human existence.

Songwriter, Shania Twain, writes about what society is most often conditioned to think of as "normal" in her 2002 song "It only hurts when I'm breathing." She sings of heartbreak and sorrow. Being human means we all feel this kind of deep pain at some point in our lives. However, using maladaptive ways of dealing with pain and suffering, I've found, only leads to more of the same. The song seems to suggest that a better way is to suppress and deny feelings rather than sit with the pain which can lead to the other side where truth and understanding exist. The lyrics go on to say that this way of coping results in freedom. From my perspective of what a best-lived life looks like, few of the words from this song are true if someone is wanting to live a life that's honoring Self. What I've found to be true of living a healthy life is to reverse the meaning of the lyrics to "It only hurts when I'm *not* breathing."

I've discovered the only way to begin my journey of healing, and to find true freedom from the adapted false self I had to become to survive my youth, was to above all else, take many deep, life giving breaths—*especially* when it hurts. A good rule for me, I've often thought, is to follow my south star, not the north star. Of course there *is* no south star. So in essence, it means to defy the norm and to instead discover what's true for me. To learn from the examples of what *not* to be. My whole being needed to shatter, not just my heart. And my dreams are my window into what my unconscious is

131

trying to encourage me to let go of. Holding on to my old adaptations of coping, mainly to *suppress* the uncomfortable, the painful, and the awkward—is to stay in bondage to the inauthentic. For me, this would be like choosing death: mind, body, and spirit.

It's taken me a long while to realize all parts exist within wholes. When I accept that everything is connected, even beginning with atoms and their relationship with protons, neutrons, and electrons, my awareness to pay attention and give care to my own parts makes sense to me. I begin to see how necessary it is.

Hope is a lived experience. Hope holds everything. Hope even has plenty of room for despair. My ability to try and unify, to integrate, primarily depends upon this understanding. And to zoom out, focusing on a more expansive view, I can claim my position and participation in the universe. Not only am I, like everyone else, having an experience *in* my universe—the universe is having an experience *through me!* I'm alive and am helping shape my world. The greatest truths come from the darkest nights of the soul. That's when I have come to the end of myself, or to the end of the self I no longer want to be. Here's the starting point. I've come to believe and trust that uncreated and unearned grace will carry me—providing there's a willingness and acceptance to understand there are no exceptions. Grace is free. And I'm choosing to live with a wise, awake heart that tries to "listen deeply to connect" to the essence of all things. I've accepted the invitation to sit at the endless table of mystery.

The time for rebirth is now. And now. And now. The process of expansion creates more and more opportunities for liberation and there is an ecstasy in paying attention. Ongoing chances to continue creating and connecting.

I am vibrant and textured; transformed and connected.

DEEP SPRINGS

"There are deep springs within each of us. Within this deep spring,
which is the very Spirit of God, is a sound. The sound of
Deep calling to Deep."

~ Miriam-Rose Ungunmerr Baumann
Indigenous educator, artist, writer,
public speaker

BIBLIOGRAPHY

Adverse Childhood Experiences (ACEs) Centers for Disease Control and Prevention: https://www.cdc.gov/violenceprevention/aces/

Branden, Nathaniel, *The Six Pillars of Self-Esteem*, Bantam Book Publishing, 1994.

Eastman, P. D., *Are You My Mother?* Random House, United States, 1960.

Genetic Sexual Attraction—Cumbria County Council: https://www.cumbria.gov.uk

Hippocratic Corpus (Oath): https://inventiongen.com/hippocratic-oath-first-do-no-harm/

Hofer, Myron Arms, M.D., *The Roots of Human Behavior: An Introduction to the Psychobiology of Early Development*, W. H. Freeman & Company, Ex-library edition, 1981.

International Cultic Studies Association, ICSA: https://icsahome.com

Laguna Beach County Water District, Laguna Beach, CA.:https://www.lbcwd.org/about-us/district-history/1993-fire-storm

Lalich, Janja, Ph.D. & Tobias, Madeleine Landau, *Take Back Your Life: Recovering from Cults and Abusive Relationships*, Audible, 2021.

Lifton, Robert J., M.D., *Thought Reform and the Psychology of Totalism*, Norton, New York, 1961.

Maté, Gabor, M.D. & Maté, Daniel, *The Myth of Normal: Trauma, Illness & Healing in a Toxic Culture*, Penguin Random House Canada, 2022.

Miriam Rose Foundation, The Dadirri Film Project (2021): https://miriamrosefoundation.org.au

BIBLIOGRAPHY

Singer, Margaret Thaler, Ph.D., *Cults in Our Midst*, Jossey-Bass, San Francisco, 2003.

Twain, Shania, music recording artist, *It Only Hurts When I'm Breathing*, 2002.

Verrier, Nancy Newton, *The Primal Wound*, Gateway Press, 1993.

HELPFUL RESOURCES

WEBSITES AND BOOKS:

Adoptee Therapist Directory: http://growbeyondwords.com

Adult Children of Alcoholics and Dysfunctional Families:
http://adultchildren.org

Adverse Childhood Experiences (ACEs): https://www.cdc. gov/violen-ceprevention

Alcoholics Anonymous 12 Step Program: https://www. aa.org

American Counseling Association/ACA: https://www.counseling.org

Code of Ethics/American Association for Marriage and Family Therapy:
https://aamft.org

DADIRRI (DA-DID-EE) Official Miriam-Rose Ungunmerr-Baumann,
YouTube Video: https://youtu.be/tow2tR_ezL8

Eye Movement Desensitization and Reprocessing Therapy (EMDR):
https://www.emdr.com

Ford (now Wolfberg), Wendy, *Recovery from Abusive Groups*, American
Family Foundation, 1993.

Fox, Bernadine, *Coming to Voice: Surviving an Abusive Therapist*, Amazon
Digital Services, LLC, 2018.

Genetic Sexual Attraction—Cumbria County Council (GSA):
https://www.cumbria.gov.uk

Hassan, Steven, Ph.D., *Freedom Of Mind Resource Center*: https: //freedomofmind.com

I Got Out: #igotout

International Cultic Studies Association (ICSA): https:// www.icsa-home.com

Kolk, Bessel V.D., M.D., *The Body Keeps The Score*, Viking Press, 2014.

Lalich, Janja, Ph.D., *International Authority on Cults and Coercion*: https:// janjalalich.com

Levin, Peter, *Waking the Tiger: Healing Trauma*, North Atlantic Books, 1997.

Lifton, Betty J., *Journey of the Adopted Self*, Basic Books, 1994.

Saving Our Sisters, Charity Organization: savingoursistersadoption.org

Schoener, Gary R., *Psychotherapists' Sexual Involvement with Clients-Intervention and Prevention*, Walk in Counseling Center, Minneapolis, 1990.

Surviving Therapist Abuse—Resources and Support for Healing: http:// www.survivingtherapistabuse.com

Therapy Link Line, (TELL), *TELLing It Like It Is: When Psychotherapists Abuse And Exploit*, Ebook, 2019: https://www.therapyabuse.org

Verrier, Nancy N., *Coming Home to Self*, Verrier Publications, 2003.

Verrier, Nancy N., *The Primal Wound*, Gateway Press, 1993.

PRIVATE FACEBOOK GROUPS:

Adoptees Connect
Adopted Chameleons
Adoptee Garage
Adoptee Trauma Support Group

Barely Rooted By Adoption
The Chameleon
Fireside Adoptees Constellation
The Gathering Place
Healing Tree: A Space For Self-Love and Self-Forgiveness
Hiraeth Hope and Healing
Psychopathic Narcissist Survivor Support Group
Reckoning With The Primal Wound
Steps To Healing After Narcissistic Abuse
Surviving Therapist Abuse
Survivors Of Adoption Memorial Resource Library
Therapist Abuse
Trauma Informed

PODCASTS:

Benn, Simon, *Thriving Adoptees*: Thriving Adoptees

Bloomberg, Wondery, *The Shrink Next Door*: The Shrink Next Door—Wondery | Premium Podcasts

Brunetti, Melissa, *Mind Your Own Karma—The Adoption Chronicles*: https://podcasts.apple.com/us/podcast/mind-your-own-karma-the-adoption-chronicles/id1592870580

Davis, Damon L., "Who Am I… Really?": https://www. whoamireallypodcast.com

Edmondson, Sarah, & Ames, Anthony "Nippy," *A Little Bit Culty*: A Little Bit Culty

Elliott, Bryan, *Living In Adoptionland*: Amazon.com: Living-adoptionland-bryan-elliot

Fox, Bernadine, *Re-Threading Madness*: RE-THREADING MADNESS

Garrard, Janeice, *Claiming Your Voice*: https://open.spotify.com/search/claimingyourvoice

Ghoston, Jennifer Dyan, *Once Upon A Time In Adopteeland*: ONCE-UPONATIME...INADOPTEELAND PODCAST

Healy, Gerard, *On The Couch*: OTC Ep. 33—Therapeutic Abuse With Amy Lynne Johnson On The Couch Podcast

Henderson, Lisa Ann, *Wandering Tree Podcast*: https:// wanderingtreepodcast.buzzsprout.com

Holden, Lori, *Adoption: The Long View*: Adoption: The Long View Podcast

Jackson, Julie Dixon, *Cut Off Genes Podcast*: CutOff Genes Investigations

Koven, Monique, *The Healing Trauma Podcast*: The Healing Trauma Podcast

Marble, Heidi, *Pulled By The Root*: https://www.pulledbytheroot.com /podcast

Medina, Amanda, *This Adoptee Life*: https://thisadopteelife.com

Radke, Haley, *Adoptees On*: https://www.adopteeson.com

Reinhardt, Sarah, & Browne, Louise, *Adoption: The Making Of Me*: Adoption

Scott, Ande, *The Adoption Files Podcast*: https://anchor.fm/ande-stanley

Shapiro, Dani, *Family Secrets*: https://danishapiro.com/family-secrets/

Syverson, Beth, Unraveling Adoption: www.unravelingadoption.com

This American Life, 2021: Trust Me I'm a Doctor—This American Life

Wiita, Carrie, & Fineman, Ben, *Very Bad Therapy: The Sociopath in the Therapy Room*: Episode 93—The Sociopath in the Therapy Room

ONLINE GROUPS AND BLOG WEBSITES:

Adoptees and Addiction: https://www.adopteesandaddiction .com

Castro, A., *Adoption Mosaic*: https://adoptionmosaic.com

Easterly, Sara, *Adoptee Voices: Supporting Adoptee Storytelling*: https://adoptee-voices.com

Gambutti, Mary, *Identity, Adoptees' Right to Know:* https://www.megam -author.com/post/adoptees-right-to-know-who-we-are?

Grubb, Lynn, *Lynn Grubb: A blog about the adoption experience*: https://noapologiesforbeingme.blogspot.com

How to Be Adopted: Improving Adoptee Wellbeing by Sharing Experiences, hosting meet-ups and campaigning for more support: https://how-tobeadopted.com (Resources for adoptees, UK based).

The Invisible Threads: https://theinvisiblethreads.com/ (LGBTQ Adoptee blog).

Joy, Lora K. My Adoptee Truth: https://www.myadoptee truth.com (Adoptee blog).

Luz, Lavender. Lori Holden author. Blog, podcast, and more: https://lavenderluz.com/

McClintock, Reshma. Dear Adoption: giving voice to those most affected by adoption: adoptees: https://dearadoption.com

McGue, Julie Ryan. This Girl. That Life: https://juliemcgueauthor.-com/solving-lifes-puzzles-with-author-emma-stevens/ (Adoptee blog).

National Association of Adoptees and Parents: https://naapunited.org (Conferences and resources).

Nordine, Janet. MS, LMFT, RPT-S. Experience Courage: https://www.ex-periencecourage.com (Therapist Adoptee blog).

Pittman, L. Adoption My Truth: A Fill-in-the-Blanks Life. 50 years in the making: https://adoptionmytruth.com (Adoptee blog).

Weatherford, Kirsten. No More Misfit: http://nomoremisfit.com (Adult Adoptee blog).

DOCUMENTARIES:

Sunderland, Paul (Lecturer) & LifeWorks: Dedicated to Recovery (Producer). 2011. *Adoption and Addiction: Remembered Not Recalled*: https://youtu.be/3e0-SsmOUJI. eecommunity

Hertzel, Michael & McClintock, Reshma (Producers). Alexander, Jeffrey & Vance, Sherie (Directors). 2019. *Calcutta is My Mother*: http://calcuttafilm.com

Frontline. WGBH Educational Foundation, 1991: My Doctor, My Lover : WGBH Educational Foundation : Free Download, Borrow, and Streaming : Internet Archive

Maté, Gabor, & Phillips, Zara, Hosted by The OLLIE Foundation, 2021. *The Trauma of Relinquishment-Adoption, Addiction, and Beyond*. Copyright Dr. Gabor Maté: https://drgabormate.com/ The Trauma of Relinquishment—Adoption, Addiction and Beyond

Sansom, Rebecca Autumn & Hawkins, Jill., PhD. (Producers). 2022. *Reckoning With The Primal Wound*. Documentary directed by Rebecca Autumn Sansom: https://reckoningwiththeprimalwound.com/

ACKNOWLEDGMENTS

For me, writing is mind-expanding. It's also how I get a visceral sense that I'm creating all the time. It's empowering. And it has been lifegiving.

My soul is full from trying to live my life in the present and in having the willingness to stay the course of what may come. So much of my life has been like experiencing wave after wave crashing into me until I didn't know which way was up. I can now say I live with the understanding that I benefit from knowing both despair and joy. Maybe this is because of too much time spent waking up in the misery caused by dead ends, or due to finally realizing I have choice. Whatever the cause, I'm joyous now, creating a life that demands my attention and requires me to stay connected to the essence of everything. I'd like to thank all parts of myself for showing up and making this possible.

My children are my joy. I love and appreciate who they are and who they are becoming. My wish is they feel so loved by themselves and others that this is something they never need to question. And if they need reassurance, I am happy to give this to them. And always with love. The kind of love that demands freedom.

A very special thanks to my daughter, who has been a Ph.D. candidate throughout the writing of both of my books. It's been thrilling to watch her go through the process of writing her dissertation. She's been my constant inspiration for all her life. Being a young wise-old-soul, she exemplifies wisdom, courage, and having a heart of compassion.

To my son, who has always shown me how to stay in the challenge to get to the other side. Even though it's often painful, awkward, and messy. Love wins.

My writing coach and fellow adoptee, Anne Heffron, has been with me through the writing of my first book *The Gathering Place: An Adoptee's Story*, and now, *A Fire Is Coming*. Anne is my lucky rabbit's foot and the best cheerleader anyone could *ever* ask for. Her ability to hear a story and offer just the right direction or possibilities to explore, is uncanny and surreal. Every time she offered a think-outside-of-the-box suggestion, I'd feel like bumping my forehead with the palm of my hand saying, *"Well, of course!"*

My editor, also a fellow adoptee, Diane Shifflett, is one of the best gifts from writing both memoirs. The kindness and compassion she has shown me has been unexpected and heartwarming. There's no one else I'd rather be inside my story with—as we analyze, repair, and polish. I have so much appreciation and gratitude for you, Diane.

My adoptee community, a group that some have titled "adopteeland," has shown strength and support, divisions and confusion, love and compassion, and how it's becoming and morphing into a new creation. I have felt the love of my community and I have loved giving my support in return. My healing journey has had a great deal to do with this group who haven't necessarily had my same experiences but are still able to say, "me too." Much love to us all.

And, to my counselors, Don and Joanna, who I have the utmost admiration and respect for. Words fail me in expressing the appreciation I have for you both. Thank you for helping me do the interior work necessary to know myself better, befriend myself, and give myself permission to choose freedom.

Emma Stevens

January 2023

ABOUT THE AUTHOR

Emma Stevens is a U.S. domestic adoptee from birth and has survived layers of trauma that have put her on multiple journeys of healing and recovery. She developed the inner strength and courage to surmount the many struggles she faced. Her traumas were born from first being relinquished and then becoming an adoptee who struggled with being forced to wear an impossible mask of playing the part of the "good adopted child."

Because of these past traumas, it's Emma's desire to be part of the movement that is dedicated to help bring forth change to the way our world views the needs and support of adopted individuals, as well as bring awareness of the exploitation that can occur by the hands of counselors, therapists, and other healthcare professionals. By sharing her experience of being exploited by her one-on-one cultic therapist, Emma is determined to expose and bring light to what an unethical, boundaryless, professional therapy situation may look like.

This memoir is Emma Stevens' second book. Her first was *The Gathering Place: An Adoptee's Story.* She has an undergraduate degree in journalism and has completed Master's level course work in psychology, specializing in Marriage, Family, and Child counseling. She has two adult children and two cat children who she adores.